Richard Webber is a journalist specialising in show-business. He has contributed to a host of newspapers and magazines and is the author of many books about classic television programmes, including the bestselling *The Complete A-Z of Dad's Army*.

Dick Clement and Ian La Frenais have forged one of the most successful writing partnerships ever seen in the entertainment business. Now based in Hollywood, Clement and La Frenais are responsible for many successful TV shows, such as *The Likely Lads* and *Auf Wiedersehen, Pet*, and numerous film scripts, including *The Commitments* and *Still Crazy*.

Porridge
The Inside Story

Richard Webber, Dick Clement
and Ian La Frenais

headline

First published in 2001
by HEADLINE BOOK PUBLISHING

First published in paperback in 2003
by HEADLINE BOOK PUBLISHING

10 9 8 7 6 5 4 3 2 1

ISBN 0 7472 3304 7

Printed and bound in Great Britain by
Mackays of Chatham plc, Chatham, Kent

Typeset in Sabon by Palimpsest Book Production Limited,
Polmont, Stirlingshire

Papers and cover board used by Headline are natural, recyclable
products made from wood grown in sustainable forests. The manufacturing processes conform to the environmental regulations of the
country of origin.

HEADLINE BOOK PUBLISHING
A division of Hodder Headline
338 Euston Road
London NW1 3BH

www.headline.co.uk
www.hodderheadline.com

To baby Hollie, whose little face has brought so much happiness

CONTENTS

ACKNOWLEDGEMENTS

I would like to thank a great number of people, all of whom have helped in various ways during the writing of this book. First of all, I'd like to thank Dick Clement and Ian La Frenais for authorising this book, for giving up time to discuss the programme and contributing to the material you're just about to read. Equally helpful have been Sydney Lotterby and Jimmy Gilbert – thanks to you both.

During the course of my research, I've spoken to many of the actors and members of the production team associated with the sitcom. For sharing memories about life at Slade Prison or *Going Straight*, thanks go to you all, especially Brian Wilde, Tony Osoba, Ken Jones, Sam Kelly, Patricia Brake, Philip Madoc, John Dair, Philip Jackson, Christopher Biggins, Paul McDowell, Terence Soall, Tony Aitken, Maurice Denham, Paul Angelis, Colin Farrell, Johnny Wade, Ray Butt, Judy Loe, Mike Crisp, Christine Walmesley-Cotham, Max Harris and Ann Ailes-Stevenson. Special thanks go to Mary Husband and Ronnie Barker, whose support and help was crucial to the success of this project.

Thanks also to Christine Dunbobbin, Rosalie Dodson, Matthew Lacey, Barbara Barrington, Allan McKeown, Rannoch Daly (for agreeing to be interviewed about making the movie at his prison, and for then writing about it as well), John Rich (for sharing memories about his American production), George Forder, Garry Morton, Peter Hunt, Chris Muzzall, everyone at Headline and, of course, my agent, Jeffrey Simmons. As always, Hilary Johnson's advice has been invaluable.

Last, but not least, I would like to acknowledge the support of my wife, Paula.

Richard Webber, July 2003

FOREWORD

by Ronnie Barker

This book is terrific – a must for all *Porridge*
aficionados. It contains information that even I didn't
know: names, dates, comments from all the actors,
even viewing figures – it's all in there. Fancy the
Christmas show 'The Desperate Hours' getting twenty
million viewers! Fancy the director in his box cursing
Fulton Mackay! Fancy Clive James fancying my
daughter Ingrid!

A mine of information – it brings it all back. What
a show. What a book.

Ronnie Barker, March 2001

'Norman Stanley Fletcher, you have pleaded guilty to the charges brought by this court and it is now my duty to pass sentence. You're a habitual criminal who accepts arrest as an occupational hazard and, presumably, accepts imprisonment in the same casual manner. We therefore feel constrained to commit you to the maximum term allowed for these offences; you will go to prison for five years.'

INTRODUCTION

Nothing else in my experience was quite as painless as *Porridge* because literally nothing went wrong. It's true we'd already done a 'one-off', where Fletcher is escorted to prison, but by its end the doors had still not slammed on him.

Once we were commissioned to write the series we visited various prisons by way of research. We had a sherry with the Governor of Brixton at the time, in the RAC Club. He was a humane, civilised man and I remember asking him what he would change about the system if he had one wish. He gave it serious thought and said he'd like to be in charge only of people who deserved to be in prison, instead of alcoholics, drug addicts or the mentally unstable.

We became profoundly depressed because there is nothing funny about the reality of prison. Then, I suppose, Fletcher started to speak to us, just as he later did to Godber. 'Bide your time, keep your nose clean. Little victories, that's what keeps you going in here.'

Later, we were in Manchester, rehearsing our stage musical, *Billy*, and writing the first series of *Porridge* in between. And we felt that since prison is about being locked up it would be less than honest not to write one episode which was set entirely in a cell. So we wrote 'A Night In', not knowing at the time that Godber would be played by the superb Richard Beckinsale. That's what I mean by nothing going wrong. Every piece of casting, for which the credit goes to Syd Lotterby, enhanced what we'd written.

This is in danger of sounding bland, but I don't remember a serious difference of opinion or a cross word. We went each week to the read-through of each episode and our main concern was ensuring that the script was the right length. Ronnie usually came up with a few embellishments and more often than not they bought their way in. Then we went away until the day of the recording. That went seamlessly and we were in the bar by nine o'clock – you don't want to hear any more of this, you want to hear about the people who loathed each other, the fights, the feuds, the tempers, the tantrums. Sorry.

Well, there was one moment in the editing room before we'd chosen a title for the series. Titles can be tricky, they either come to you or they don't. Ronnie came in and announced that he'd got the perfect one. 'So have we!' we countered. A heated argument ensued for about ten seconds until we settled who was to go first. Ronnie won the coin toss. 'Porridge!' he announced triumphantly. 'That's our title!' we said. 'Swear to God!' End of debate, dispute over, off to the bar.

Dick Clement

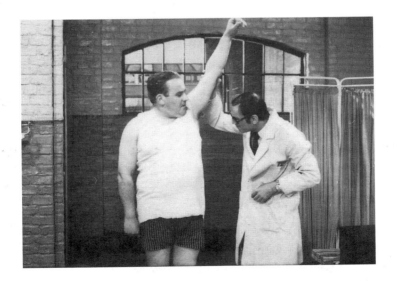

THE PILOT

It's New Year's Eve and Fletcher is transferred from Brixton to Slade Prison, situated miles from anywhere in the wilderness of Cumberland. Sharing a train compartment with Mr Mackay and Mr Barrowclough, who'll become his greatest foes while serving his five-year prison sentence, he heads north for another spell behind bars.

To help while the time away, Barrowclough strikes up a conversation with Fletcher during which he explains that Slade is an experimental prison, regarded as a provider of 'sympathy and understanding' rather than of 'correction and punishment' – not that you would think so, with the bellowing Mackay around.

After disembarking at a rural station, Fletcher is in such desperate need of a toilet that he's told to relieve himself around the back of the van. Little do the warders know that it's all a cunning plan: Fletch, always the opportunist, urinates into the van's petrol tank!

En route to the prison, high on the moors, the minibus breaks down. With darkness closing in, Mackay sets off for help while Fletcher remains handcuffed to Barrowclough in the van. As the temperature drops, Fletcher puts the frighteners on Barrowclough by claiming they'll perish if they don't find somewhere warm. He persuades the weak-willed warder to shelter in a nearby deserted cottage, where they toast the New Year with a hot drink topped up with Scotch courtesy of Mackay's pocket!

While Fletcher keeps plying him with drink, a gloom-laden Barrowclough discusses life's sorrows and eventually agrees to release the handcuffs. But when the prison warder nods off, Fletcher grasps the opportunity to escape into the night. After hours on the run, he breaks into an empty cottage only to find he's back where he started!

'Prisoner and Escort' was one instalment from a set of pilots transmitted by the BBC in a search for a new comedy vehicle for Ronnie Barker. The project – titled *Seven of One* – was steered from its inception by executive producer Jimmy Gilbert and was part of a larger-scale project instigated when the BBC secured the services of Ronnie Barker and Ronnie Corbett from London Weekend Television. 'They were both promised a light-entertainment show, a Special each, plus a scripted comedy each, and *Seven of One* was the way of finding a situation comedy for Ronnie Barker,' explains Jimmy.

To ensure he received top-quality scripts, he turned to writers he knew. 'I commissioned more than the seven I needed. Two came from Roy Clarke, two from Clement and La Frenais, two from Hugh Leonard, one from a writer called Gerald Frow – which Yorkshire later made into a series with Clive Dunn – one written by Ronnie Barker himself, and one from N. F. Simpson.' Having selected those he wanted to pursue, Jimmy – with the help of his directors, Harold Snoad and Sydney Lotterby – put them into production.

One of the ideas submitted by Dick Clement and Ian La Frenais was based on life in prison, a theme largely untested in the genre of situation comedy and one that some people doubted had the staying power required for a long-running show. The show's chief player, Ronnie Barker, didn't share such doubts. He had always wanted to develop the idea of a prison-based show. 'When I was preparing a previous set of pilots I'd recorded, *Six Dates with Barker* – from which *The Phantom Raspberry-Blower* originated and was developed into a serial for *The Two Ronnies* – I'd write down various situations as ideas. One of these jottings simply said 'prison'; I always wanted to make a prison series and couldn't believe it when I spoke to Dick and Ian and discovered they'd come up with a similar idea.

'They were thinking, initially, about an open prison but I didn't think that had enough threat to it, whereas my idea was much more frivolous than *Porridge* – like *Bilko* in prison: smuggling women in, that sort of thing.'

Clement and La Frenais had built their success in sitcom around scripts containing more realism than Ronnie's idea afforded, so after a little deliberating they agreed on a closed

4

prison – a setting in which the writers could exploit the daily dilemmas facing inmates. Ronnie was happy with Dick and Ian's desire to write something with a degree of reality. 'It was definitely the best way to go because my idea would have been geared much more towards laughs, whereas theirs possessed more bite.'

It was a judicious move to focus on the realism of the chosen situation. This allowed Clement and La Frenais the freedom – particularly during the actual series – to probe not only moments of grim reality for the prisoners of Slade Prison but compensatory elements too, such as the emergence of Fletcher as a father figure for young Godber.

When the writers sat down to pen the pilot, the script took off in an unexpected direction, as Dick Clement explains. 'We started writing the piece for Ronnie and found we couldn't stop; it went beyond just one episode and before we knew it we'd written an entire series.'

'It wasn't about a guy in prison, but about someone who'd just come out only to find his wife was having an affair with his best friend. Before long, we had written about fifty pages based on this situation, and envisaged Ronnie being the ex-prisoner. As we knew we had an entire series here, we put it aside,' adds Ian La Frenais.

Knowing they had exceeded Jimmy Gilbert's original requirements, Clement and La Frenais titled the scripts *Thick as Thieves* and sold the series to LWT. 'Meantime, Ronnie was still expecting something about prison, so we sat down and wrote "Prisoner and Escort". Later on, people asked why we were so obsessed with criminality, but it was just a coincidence: we set out to write a script for Ronnie but soon realised there was more than one episode in the idea.'

Clement and La Frenais didn't experience any difficulties writing the pilot script, and enjoyed the process. 'It was enormous fun,' says Ian. 'Once we'd established the main character in our minds, we were away. Of course, it helped knowing you were writing for Ronnie Barker – after all, he was so popular. We knew that if we didn't screw it up we had a real chance of success.'

As soon as Sydney Lotterby, who directed 'Prisoner and Escort', saw the pilot script, he knew they were on to a winner. 'It was wonderful and just pleading to be done – it was so clever. The script revealed the essence of Dick and Ian's writing: they don't write gags; they write situations and explore the personalities of the characters, which is why they score so well. Their scripts contain character and situation jokes, not just gags. With *Porridge*, their work was very accurate and seemed to reveal how a prisoner felt – it's almost as if they'd experienced prison life themselves!'

Casting for 'Prisoner and Escort', as well as for the other pilots, was Jimmy Gilbert's responsibility. In addition to Fletcher, the two main characters in the script were Mr Mackay and Mr Barrowclough. 'It was Ronnie's idea to recruit Brian Wilde to play Barrowclough,' explains Jimmy. 'He'd worked with him before, I believe, but I'd also known Brian from my RADA days. Ronnie thought he'd be marvellous in it and, of course, he was absolutely right.'

Jimmy Gilbert, meanwhile, knew Fulton Mackay. Since studying at drama school together, and then working at Glasgow's Citizens' Theatre as actors in the early 1950s, they'd become good friends. Jimmy recalls: 'It was whilst serving in India that he met a sergeant who pulled his neck in a funny way – something he later copied while playing Mr Mackay. I directed a series with Terry-Thomas, and Fulton played a similar character – a colonial sergeant in the police. He was great in that, so when the part of the prison warder – who by sheer coincidence was also called Mackay – came up, he was my first choice.'

Fletcher plies the joyless
Mr Barrowclough
with alcohol

But before offering the part to his old friend, Jimmy Gilbert contacted Clement and La Frenais. 'It's important you involve the writers because you don't want to suddenly find they've got a phobia about somebody. So I rang Dick and said: "How about Fulton Mackay for the part of Mackay?" Dick replied: "He'd be marvellous but do you think he'd do it?" I thought Fulton would be interested, so gave him a copy of the script and he jumped at the chance.'

The casting was spot-on. 'The three of them [Ronnie Barker, Fulton Mackay and Brian Wilde] worked well together, and they had great respect for each other,' says Jimmy. 'Brian – with his wonderful put-upon demeanour – and Fulton were the perfect balance for each other. There's a wonderful selection of characters in *Porridge* that are realistic and different. It was the same with Fulton: he brought something of his own personality to the role; he created this totally real authoritarian character. He was so funny.'

Because the pilot script centred on the transfer of Fletcher to the remote Cumberland prison, location shooting had to be organised. Jimmy Gilbert had already travelled to Wales to record 'I'll Fly You for A Quid' and knew immediately the location was ideal for 'Prisoner and Escort', despite the script being set mainly in Cumberland. 'I thought that the hills above the valleys of Caerphilly resembled the north of England; and, as the area was easy to reach, we ended up filming all the moorland scenes for "Prisoner and Escort" there.' Jimmy enjoyed making the pilot. 'I remember watching the filming and thinking how funny the scenes were, even though, at that point, they hadn't been pieced together.'

Ronnie Barker, meanwhile, recalls the inclement weather they endured while filming. 'It was terribly cold, which wasn't ideal because I did a lot of running across the moors; but then, I always remember cold weather whenever I think about BBC filming!' Overall, Ronnie was pleased with how the pilot panned out. 'The filming was successful, it was well shot and the reaction from the audience when we recorded the studio scenes was excellent.'

One of the scenes from the pilot is classed as among the 'finest memories' for writer Dick Clement. As he explains: 'It's when Fletcher escapes from the cottage, wanders around all night and breaks into a building; we had to conceal from the audience the fact that he was back in the same place – otherwise we wouldn't have got the laugh – which Sydney did superbly.'

Working alongside Sydney Lotterby as production manager was Ray Butt, who remained part of the team for the first series of *Porridge*. As production manager, his responsibilities involved finding locations. 'On a new programme, where nothing has been established, you're looking for one key location. Once found, you try to find any other locations nearby, so you're not travelling all the time.'

The series of pilots was successful in finding not one but two hit shows for Ronnie Barker: while 'Prisoner and Escort' was commissioned and re-titled *Porridge*, Roy Clarke's 'Open All Hours' kept its name and later became a successful series for the comedy actor. There was a third script Ronnie would like to have progressed. Written by Clement and La Frenais, 'I'll Fly You for a Quid' focussed on a Welsh gambling family who'd have a flutter on anything. 'It started off with them gambling on how long the sermon would last at church. It was an excellent script.'

The decision regarding which pilot would be made into a full-blown series was made at a restaurant. Around the table were Jimmy Gilbert, Duncan Wood (then Head of Comedy) and Ronnie Barker. They chewed over the merits of each show until two were left in the frame: 'Prisoner and Escort' and 'I'll Fly You for a Quid'. While Ronnie was keen on the latter, Jimmy Gilbert felt the idea lacked the stamina to survive. He says: 'It was a perfect short story but I couldn't see beyond the pilot.'

Jimmy and Duncan Wood favoured 'Prisoner and Escort', although they knew the writers were initially unsure how they could develop the situation into an on-going series. 'I thought "Prisoner and Escort" was tremendous in every way, and with Brian Wilde and Fulton Mackay it was really a three-hander,' says Jimmy. But he appreciated the task facing Clement and La Frenais. 'Not only did they have to place them all inside prison, but also what had been a tightly scripted and plotted pilot had to be expanded to include many more characters.'

When Clement and La Frenais were consulted about the decision to develop 'Prisoner and Escort' into a series, they felt the right choice had been made. 'I think it had the edge on "I'll Fly You for A Quid",' says Dick. 'Somebody once said that sitcom is all about a captive situation – and you can't get more captive than prison!'

Initial transmission: 📺 **Sunday 1 April 1973 BBC2, 8.15 p.m.**

CAST

Norman Fletcher . . . . **Ronnie Barker**
Mr Barrowclough . . . . **Brian Wilde**
Mr Mackay . . . . **Fulton Mackay**
Prison Warder . . . . **Hamish Roughead**

PRODUCTION TEAM

Written by . . . . **Dick Clement
and Ian La Frenais**
Music . . . . **Max Harris**
Film Cameraman . . . . **Alan Featherstone**
Film Editor . . . . **Ray Millichope**
Make-up . . . . **Penny Delamar**
Costume . . . . **Penny Lowe**
Lighting . . . . **Peter Smee**
Sound . . . . **Mike McCarthy**
Design . . . . **Tim Gleeson**
Executive Producer . . . . **James Gilbert**
Producer/Director . . . . **Sydney Lotterby**

WHAT A SCENE!

**During the train journey to Slade Prison, Fletcher gives
Mackay lip and is warned not to try it on.**

FLETCHER
I wouldn't, Mr Mackay, I wouldn't, would I? Otherwise
you'll wait till the train gets a bit of speed up outside Hemel
Hempstead and chuck me out the window, wouldn't you?
Put it down on the official report as attempted escape.

BARROWCLOUGH
He wouldn't do that.

FLETCHER
No, s'pose not . . . he couldn't spell Hemel Hempstead, he'd
wait till we got to Rugby.

MACKAY
Now look! (Clenching his fist) I'm a reasonable man, but one
more allegation of brutality and I'm going to let you have it.

Seven of One

The series was made up of seven pilots and transmitted on BBC2 between 25 March and 6 May 1973.

1. **'Open All Hours' (written by Roy Clarke)**

2. **'Prisoner and Escort' (written by Dick Clement and Ian La Frenais)**

3. **'My Old Man' (written by Gerald Frow)**

4. **'Spanner's Eleven' (written by Roy Clarke)**

5. **'Another Fine Mess' (written by Hugh Leonard)**

6. **'One Man's Meat' (written by Jack Goetz, alias Ronnie Barker)**

7. **'I'll Fly You for a Quid' (written by Dick Clement and Ian La Frenais)**

MAKING *PORRIDGE*

Porridge was more than a sitcom: it was comedy drama of the highest order, played out in a claustrophobic environment that exuded a degree of tension Clement and La Frenais could exploit. Inmates, locked away with their freedom held in the hands of others and forced to bide their time with all sorts of unsavoury individuals, were rich veins of conflict just waiting to be tapped, as Messrs Clement and La Frenais discovered. And the scriptwriters made the most of their golden opportunity, delivering script after script of crisp, inventive writing, epitomised beautifully in the episode 'A Night In'. The entire episode centres on Fletcher and Godber locked up in their cell, with the young, first-time offender confiding in the more experienced lag, unveiling his fears and anxieties concerning surviving life inside. The episode contains many poignant moments, with Fletch, an emerging father figure for young Godber, dishing out advice on how to survive prison. In this momentary expression of humanity, human frailties and kindness are exposed in a fine display of just how subtle and rewarding Clement and La Frenais' comedy can be.

Glowing radiantly like a beacon, *Porridge* outshone its rivals in this congested genre of British television. The twenty scripts brought to life on screen between September 1974 and March 1977 were of a striking quality, so it is surprising to learn that Clement and La Frenais initially questioned whether they could extract enough humour from the grim setting of Slade Prison. 'We visited Brixton Prison and met with the governor, but after being shown around the place felt really deflated, thinking we'd definitely picked the wrong pilot from the *Seven of One* series to pursue,' admits Ian.

'We also visited Wormwood Scrubs and Wandsworth Prison,' adds Dick. 'We became very daunted: writing "Prisoner and Escort" was one thing, but we came out of the prisons and said to each other: "How the hell do we make a whole series based in prison funny?" At the end of the day, prisons are grim and we knew our show also had to reflect that; it would have been dishonest and cheap to trivialise it, thereby not dealing with the fact that it really is a heavy place.' Clement and La Frenais purposely addressed such truths early on in series one – with 'A Night In'. 'The one thing you could do on TV, probably better than any other medium, was to have an entire episode set inside a cell. Prison is about being locked up, so we decided to do this episode early on as a way of facing the fact that prison isn't funny: Lennie being scared and depressed reflected the harshness of the situation.'

The next stage in their research was pivotal in ridding their minds of the lingering doubt about their ability to make a prison-based sitcom entertaining. Realism and humour go hand in hand in Clement and La Frenais' work, yet the dearth of humorous moments found during their research visits to real-life prisons concerned them. Key players in helping show them the light were Jonathan Marshall and Jimmy Gilbert. 'At first, Dick and Ian felt it would be difficult to open up the story,' recalls Jimmy, 'so I referred them to Jonathan, who'd been introduced to me by a neighbour. He'd just written a book – which was later published – titled *How to Survive in the Nick*, and agreed to meet with Dick and Ian.'

Clement and La Frenais remember sitting down for a drink in Richmond and discussing prison life with Marshall. 'Just talking about the routine of prison life was valuable,' says Dick. 'In terms of providing the kind of basic information you need before you can start writing a series, Jonathan was a great help.'

'He taught us a lot about the slang used in prison,' says Ian, 'and was helpful in providing plenty of hints. But the hardest thing was how to work a plot in such a small, enclosed captive world each week, where the parameters are so tight; this is why the show turned out more character-driven than most series.'

A phrase uttered by Marshall focussed the writers' minds and injected a grain of optimism, as Ian recalls. 'Jonathan started telling us stories about being inside and kept using the phrase "little victories", which struck a chord. Dick and I thought that maybe this was the key: we could make the show about a man with a fondness for earning "little victories" – beating the system on a daily basis, even in the most trivial ways.'

That everyday survival had become the driving force of the show that

Designer Tim Gleeson built a remarkable set at Ealing Film Studios

encouraged Clement and La Frenais enough to begin writing the first episode, 'New Faces, Old Hands'. This they undertook from a Manchester hotel room: their successful stage musical *Billy* was playing in the city, prior to its move to London's Drury Lane; between rehearsals, they returned to the Midland Hotel and worked on the *Porridge* scripts.

As soon as the scripts started arriving at Television Centre, producer Sydney Lotterby and Jimmy Gilbert were impressed with what they saw. 'Their writing had it all,' says Jimmy. 'Dick might have been more into plot, and Ian into dialogue, but they were the perfect partnership. Dick, being a director – and a very good one – thought visually; he knew what the medium was all about.'

Although he'd enjoyed the pilot, Sydney Lotterby had doubted whether the idea for a prison-based sitcom was sufficiently strong to carry an entire series – until he got his

Fletcher carried a lot of influence within the walls of Slade Prison

hands on the scripts. 'A director's job, and an actor's, is easy when you receive quality scripts because all you're doing is interpreting something you know is right. Your job is much more difficult if the scripts aren't of a high standard: that's when everyone pulls out the stops to make it work. But making bad scripts work is difficult.'

Appointing Sydney to direct the series was welcomed by all quarters. Jimmy Gilbert, the man who recruited Lotterby to the team, regarded him as a 'most excellent director, who directed for total reality'. Meanwhile Dick Clement and Ian La Frenais felt reassured that someone they respected and with whom they had worked before (Lotterby had helped Clement through his first piece of small-screen directing, *The Likely Lads*) was at the helm.

'I was delighted Sydney was directing the series,' explains Dick, 'and I think it was his finest work. Take, for example, 'A Night In', from the first series, where Sydney was challenged with making an entire half-hour television comedy inside a prison cell. He didn't let that put him off and found every possible way to shoot two people in a small cell. He shot it brilliantly and never missed a trick; he cast all the parts beautifully, too. We were thrilled to have him on the show.'

Ian La Frenais also has nothing but gratitude for Sydney steering the show along. 'I admired him enormously and knew that, providing we didn't screw up and become sloppy with the scripts, *Porridge* was in safe hands.'

Ronnie Barker, too, was pleased with the choice of director. 'Sydney is a very gentle, calm character, and we never had rows or shouted at each other. He's an experienced director, which showed in how he went about his work.'

Creating the Characters

When the BBC commissioned the first series, Dick Clement and Ian La Frenais knew they had three characters already in place.

Fletcher, Mackay and Barrowclough had all featured in 'Prisoner and Escort', but the writers were keen to create one more main character, as Ian explains. 'We wanted a newcomer to prison, a guy who could act as our audience in many ways, allowing Fletch to become a sort of mentor.' In doing so, all the slang, procedures and general information about prisons that the writers wanted to impart could be conveyed through Fletcher. 'You can only do that by telling someone who's scared and never been inside before. If both Fletch and Godber were old lags they wouldn't have had those conversations, but with Fletch explaining everything to a newcomer we were able to deliver all these facts in a digestible way.'

One influence behind the series' central character, Fletcher, came from a book – a Czech classic Dick had picked up. 'It sounds slightly pretentious – and I'm not even sure I read the whole book – but it was about a man not dissimilar to Fletcher, in that he was at the bottom of the totem pole but survived by his wits and was, in a way, indefatigably cheerful: somebody whose attitude was all about "getting by".'

The nearest the writers came to meeting a real-life Fletcher was in America, while they were conducting research for the American version, *On the Rocks*, which ran to twenty-three episodes on ABC and was shown between 1975 and 1976.

Dick recalls the moment. 'We started to do the American version before we'd finished the English show, so we were visiting American prisons and carrying out research while still writing series three for the UK. This prisoner, who turned out to be a murderer, had similar attitudes to Fletcher. One of the guards said: "He never gives us any bother because he isn't a repeat offender." And they'd made him the prison photographer – which explained why he followed us around taking very inept photographs. Finding a cushy number like that was exactly what Fletcher would have done. He had all the cheeriness of Fletcher, too.'

While they queued in this prison's canteen, Clement and La Frenais experienced a scene that could have been lifted directly from a *Porridge* script. 'We were in the food line, trying to choose what we wanted, when someone said that we were only allowed one piece of chicken. At that moment, the guy serving the food gave me an extra bit.' This was an entirely cussed action, yet another attempt to beat the system in any way possible, and something the writers viewed as an attitude familiar in *Porridge*.

When Clement and La Frenais created Fletcher, they already knew that Ronnie Barker would play their character; this partly influenced the way they developed the old lag. 'Ronnie is a brilliant comic actor and approached the part totally from an actor's point of view, rather than wanting us to write a star vehicle for him,' recalls Dick.

Representative of the establishment were the ineffectual Mr Barrowclough and the inimitable Mr Mackay, both created (along with Norman Fletcher) for the pilot episode. 'They were a great contrast: one was a total bastard who you had to watch out for at every moment, the other a pushover,' remarks Dick. 'You could play one against the other, and it seemed logical to have two characters like that.'

Clement and La Frenais admit they didn't appreciate the true potential of the characters until the first series was in the can and they had time to reflect. Ian says: 'We underused them throughout the first series, not realising just how good they were – particularly Mr Mackay.' But he understands why this happened. 'We were still trying to find Fletcher, as well as establishing Godber, so developing other characters took time.'

Dick concedes that another reason they didn't capitalise on the likes of Mackay was because they didn't spend much time beforehand thinking their characters through. 'Nowadays, people writing sitcoms spend ages analysing their characters before putting pen to paper; that way, they can establish who's important and make sure they're given a fair share of the lines. But we were writing by the seat of our pants! We should have known by looking at the pilot that Mr Mackay in particular was going to be an asset, because he was absolutely brilliant.' Dick adds, however, 'We may have underused him at the start, but gradually gave him more and more to do.'

As Mackay got stronger, the importance of Mr Barrowclough somewhat dimmed. This was disappointing for actor Brian Wilde, who played the warder, especially because the character had been so prominent in the pilot. 'In many ways, I don't think that character had anywhere to go,' says Dick, 'whereas Mr Mackay's did, because it was richer.'

When it came to finding names for the series' protagonists, Dick and Ian's past came into play. Just as for many of their other shows, particularly *The Likely Lads*, names weren't necessarily plucked from thin air. Lennie Godber stemmed from the writers' London-based hairdresser, Denny Godber, while Dick had a close friend, Norman Stanley Gordon, whose name was adapted and became Norman Stanley Fletcher. 'We also wanted a name you could abbreviate, and Fletch sounded good,' says Ian.

It was pure coincidence that the writers picked the surname Mackay for a character to be played by his name-sake Fulton Mackay, and Mr Barrowclough was a name that simply sounded right, as Dick explains. 'It sounds like a northern name, which is what we wanted, and there was a lovely rhythm to the phrase: "Pull yourself together, Mr Barrowclough!" You have to experiment with names and see how they sound in certain situations – and they all seemed fine to us.'

'I like the name Barrowclough,' adds Ian. 'It's a wonderfully old-fashioned kind of East Riding name. It was the name of a Newcastle footballer and of a street in the Newcastle area, but I don't know of anyone in particular that could have influenced our choice.'

Another decision Clement and La Frenais faced when the series was commissioned was what to call the sitcom. 'Prisoner and Escort' was apposite for the pilot, but hardly suited the programme once Fletcher arrived at Slade Prison. The importance of a suitable-sounding title cannot be under-estimated, but making a decision wasn't easy, as Ian explains. 'We toyed with one or two, then thought about words like "stir" and "inside", from which the word *Porridge* emerged; at first, it seemed a bit daft, but the more we thought about it, the more it grew on us.'

But they weren't the only ones to come up with that title. Dick recalls: 'We were with Ronnie Barker, who said: "By the way, I've got a title." I replied: "So have we." He told us *Porridge*, and we said: "My God – that's the same as ours!" Quite independently we'd come up with the same title. It's obviously a slang term but it's just one word, which is desirable, and immensely memorable.'

Many noteworthy characters were seen during the sitcom's run, including Grouty – expertly played by Peter Vaughan – and Judge Rawley, brought to life briefly by veteran character actor Maurice Denham. Clement and La Frenais were equally adept at creating supplementary characters. 'The idea behind Grouty was that he's the enemy within,' explains Dick. 'Your enemy is not just the screws but also other prisoners, as any prison series or movie will tell you. You're just as scared of the people within as you are of the authorities, so when we wrote 'The Harder They Fall' we felt it was about time we introduced Grouty. Peter Vaughan created a very sinister yet funny prisoner who became a huge addition to the team.'

The idea to introduce the judge responsible for sentencing Fletcher evolved from the scripts Clement and La Frenais had written for the American version. As Dick recalls: 'The American TV company wanted twenty-three scripts in a year,

and when we'd run out of adapting *Porridge* scripts we had
to write new episodes. When it came to writing series three
for the UK, we used storylines that had been completed in
the States. We were constantly translating material that had
been used in the States for the UK, whereas earlier we had
adapted the British scripts for the American market – it was
an extraordinary situation.'

Casting

Although three of the main characters for *Porridge* had
already been placed for the pilot, 'Prisoner and Escort', a
host of prisoners and warders had to be recruited to occupy
Slade Prison. So, with the scripts complete, Sydney Lotterby's
mind turned to casting the remaining team, and it was with
his assistant, Judy Loe, that he set about the task. Judy
worked alongside Sydney Lotterby for more than thirty years,
initially as his production secretary and later as a production
assistant. She was involved in all sorts of duties connected
with *Porridge*, including running the production office. 'I'd
normally be the first person to work with the producer on
the programme, before anyone else joined the team,' Judy
explains. 'I was involved in everything from getting the
scripts typed to arranging the casting.' Judy has nothing but
happy memories of working on *Porridge*. 'It was enjoyable
and everyone got on well together – it was a nice little unit.'

Of those roles left to fill, the most important was that of
naïve first offender Lennie Godber. To do this, Ronnie Barker
suggested Paul Henry, who made his name playing woolly-hatted
Benny in *Crossroads*. 'I'd just worked with him, and thought he
was well suited for the role, but Sydney wanted Richard
Beckinsale. I remember him saying to me: "I think this chap
Richard Beckinsale, who's done *The Lovers*, would be good –
have a look at this tape of the show." Sydney thought Richard
was right for the part because of his sensitivity as an actor.'

Ronnie kept an open mind and watched the tape: he was
impressed with what he saw and had no objections to
Beckinsale being offered the role. It wasn't long before he

knew the director had made the right choice. 'It was the first time I'd worked with Richard and as soon as we'd finished the read-through I knew Sydney was correct to suggest him.'

It was imperative that the principal actors worked well together, especially as most of the action was played out in the confines of a tiny cell; where such a restrictive environment would magnify the interplay between the actors, any underlying weaknesses or incompatibilities would stick out like a sore thumb. But there were no such worries on the set of *Porridge* because Ronnie knew immediately that he'd form a fruitful working relationship with Richard. 'Very rarely have I worked with someone I hate; it makes the job a hundred times more difficult. In *The Two Ronnies* people would comment on the fact we were using the same people, but with such a short rehearsal-time you've got to know from day one that whoever you're working with will know his lines, is reliable and a nice guy.

'I sensed the comedian in Richard straight away; it was like working with David Jason – a riot from start to finish. Richard was very funny and his comic timing impeccable; I loved working with him.' Although Beckinsale grew restless with the 'innocent young male roles' he was increasingly offered, and despite the character of Godber being just as young and easily led as others he'd played, Ronnie never noticed any concerns regarding the role. Perhaps this was because *Porridge* was more solemn than other sitcoms he'd worked on. 'I never felt he wanted to do anything more serious, or pithy,' says Ronnie.

'He had such a facility for being sympathetic and playing the naïve characters, although in real life he wasn't, of course. You could sense all the mothers saying: "Aah, isn't he sweet." He just exuded charm, his timing was excellent and he had a great sense of fun.'

Sydney had seen Richard in several shows and knew he'd be perfect as Godber. 'He was just right, although initially he had trouble with the Birmingham accent. Just like the scar on Fletcher's chin in the early episodes, the Brummie accent got lost and we finally settled for a Nottingham accent, which is where Richard was born.'

Clement and La Frenais acknowledge the part Sydney Lotterby played in making *Porridge* one of the BBC's most successful sitcoms. 'He cast the original pilot beautifully, then later recruited Richard and all the other key players – it was a fantastic piece of work.' Dick remembers Sydney calling to tell them about bringing Richard Beckinsale into the fold. 'We admired Richard so much, and Sydney was casting higher than our original expectations, which was fine with us. We hadn't really seen the part of Lennie being that big, but, once Beckinsale had been cast, he was so damned good and bonded so well with Ronnie that we just wanted to use him more and more.'

Dick considers the qualities Beckinsale brought to the role injected into it an enormous humanity and believability. 'He was also very honest and appealing, which helped as well because one found oneself on his side. There was an unmistakable truth in his acting, even though he was a terrible reader at the read-throughs,' says Dick, with a smile. 'The rest of the cast, who knew what he was like, would almost groan if they knew he had a long speech because they had to sit through his stuttering; he was a lousy reader and we used to joke about how the hell he got his first job! But during the four days' rehearsal everything always came together, and his performance during the recording was almost effortless, as well as wonderfully true.'

Ian La Frenais, too, was surprised and taken aback when he first heard Richard read. 'He was hopeless. He'd sit there, look at the script and give the most terrible reading. But he was always very laid back, knew he was a bad reader and had confidence in his own abilities to make sure he was word-perfect for the first run-through on the floor – and was.

'Despite all of that, the chemistry between Richard and Ronnie was wonderful. Richard was a rising young performer, a unique talent, while Ronnie was the master. A lot of actors are uncomfortable with that strange hybrid of activity and television with an audience; it's a bit strange and unnerving for many actors, but Ronnie loved it.'

'Ronnie was a pure genius,' says Dick. 'He always brought little additions to the scripts. At the read-throughs he'd always throw in an extra ad-lib and ask: "Is that all right?" He wanted the laugh but not if it was a cheap laugh or out of character. He was wonderfully funny and had such a quick brain, which was ideal because Fletcher was a man who lived by his wits. We needed a man who was quick on his feet, with a lively mind, and Ronnie was right for the role. He was a joy to work with and not in any way a selfish actor.'

Dick and Ian were also happy with the casting of Fulton Mackay and Brian Wilde, who carried their characters forward from 'Prisoner and Escort'. 'I adored Fulton, he was one of my favourite human beings in the world – and I still miss him,' comments Dick. 'Syd used to say Fulton never wanted to stop rehearsing, he would go on forever. But what came with that was this wonderful enthusiasm: he loved what he was doing, so you didn't mind that foible one little bit. He was a perfectionist, working away all the time, and you knew he was after the best performance he could possibly achieve. I saw a lot of his work and thought he was fantastic; he was an enormously well rounded human being, an interesting man who could strike up a conversation about anything.

Christopher Biggins, David Jason, Ronnie Barker and Richard Beckinsale act out a perfect scene

'Brian, meanwhile, brought something wonderfully lugubrious to his character, which was slightly reminiscent of Robb Wilton: I remember him from my childhood and his misery was funny. Rather like Captain Mainwaring in *Dad's Army*, Mr Barrowclough had a terrible marriage, and the way Fletcher exploited him was funny.'

Plenty of other established actors were spotted in Slade Prison, including David Jason, who went on to work with Ronnie Barker in another hit show, *Open All Hours*. 'An older character, called Blanco, was created,' says Sydney Lotterby, 'and as soon as Ronnie saw the script he said: "That's a part for David Jason." I replied: "Who?" David wasn't a big name then, and was also a young man, so when he turned up I was worried we'd made the wrong choice.' But as soon as make-up was applied and Jason started performing, Sydney was able to relax. 'He did terribly well; he's such an accomplished performer, and had worked with Ronnie before, which helped.'

Another character, Judge Rawley, was played by veteran stage- and screen-actor Maurice Denham. Sydney recalls that he fitted in well and was very conscientious about his performance, and production manager Mike Crisp also enjoyed working with him. 'It was a happy experience; Maurice was a very sweet man and well liked by the entire cast,' he says. Mike remembers the day he met a real-life judge with the same name. 'One of the first things a production manager does as soon as he receives a script is to make sure – where possible – that there isn't a person with the same name.

'Normally this is a job that would be farmed out to the reference library, although it remains the production manager's responsibility. Similarly, if someone gives out a phone number in the script, it has to be a dead line. When I saw there was a character called Judge Rawley in the script, I got the library to check; I was told there wasn't a judge with that name, so didn't think any more about it.'

It was six weeks before the cast recorded the episode in the studio. 'After an incident-free recording, I noticed a

Veteran actor Maurice Denham played Judge Rawley, a friend of the Governor Mr Venables (the late Michael Barrington)

very distinguished man standing at the bottom of the audience rostrum,' continues Mike. 'It turned out he was with his son, and he said to me: "Oh, Mr Crisp, I would just like to say how much my son and I have enjoyed tonight's performance." When he introduced himself, I nearly fell through the floor because the judge was his namesake! It was an understandable mistake, because his surname was spelt differently to the one we'd checked, and fortunately he didn't mind.'

Authenticity is always important, even in situation comedy, and Mike, who worked on a Christmas Special and the third series, was keen to ensure this was achieved. 'I did some research and discovered that most prisoners are aged between eighteen and thirty and representative of an ethnic mix, whereas the people used as extras in the series were all old lag look-alikes – mainly white and aged between fifty and sixty. When I took over, I changed all that and brought in a range of people to play non-speaking roles. Overall, I think it worked well.'

Set-building

It was hoped that most interior scenes would be shot inside a real jail, but plans fell through at the eleventh hour. This was when Tim Gleeson, an experienced designer who had worked at the BBC since 1957, was summoned. Tim is now retired from the Beeb, but during his time there worked on many hit shows, including *Keeping Up Appearances* and *Yes, Minister*. When he became involved with *Porridge*, he was familiar with the show, having been the designer on 'Prisoner and Escort' and other pilots in the *Seven of One* series, but the requirements in this instance were much greater than anything previously tackled. While prison cells and offices could be filmed in the BBC studios, the association area – where the prisoners gather to play games or watch television, and where Fletcher is seen walking along to his cell in the opening credits – was too large for any studio at Television Centre. Sydney Lotterby had to put his thinking cap on.

Tim recalls the moment he was asked to help. 'Time was slipping away and Syd said: "Tim, we're desperate, is there any way we can conjure up a multilevel prison at Ealing Studios?" The timescale involved was incredibly short – it was only weeks until he wanted to start filming – so everything became telescoped.

'Magically, I discovered there was an old tank at Ealing, which was used for underwater filming-sequences and any other scenes involving water. The tank enabled me to build a multilevel structure. When you built scenery there was an accepted rule that no individual item could be made that two men couldn't handle, which was reasonable because everything had to be carried on and off trucks, up and down stairs, in and out of the studio. But it's not always easy, especially when you're faced with building walkways that have to bear the weight of several people.

'The tank itself was about nine feet deep, but by good fortune I was able to cantilever the walkways out over the top of it. Two thirds of the entire structure were fixed to the studio floor, allowing the other third to project outwards.'

All location shots for each series were done together, usually during a week's filming at Ealing Studios, after which the structure was dismantled. However, certain episodes contained scenes that necessitated the reassembling of segments of the construction within the studio. 'Some shots required the association area and the gantry suspended above, although no one would walk on it,' explains Tim.

No one can underestimate the magnitude of the task he faced. 'It was a massive job,' he admits, 'probably one of the most difficult I've designed, considering the timescale involved and the lack of co-operation from the authorities, which meant I was prevented from modelling the set on a real prison.

'As well as constructing the set, we also had to make it look realistic. We probably made the prison look dirtier than it perhaps would have been in real life.' Tim and his team used a technique know as 'blowing down': after the scenery has been built, a coat of paint is applied to it; the painters then delicately apply a light layer of dark-grey liquid spray. This produces an instantly aged effect, making the scenery appear old and worn.

Sydney Lotterby was enamoured of Tim's achievements at Ealing. 'Fletch's cell and the association area were relatively straightforward, but sometimes I wanted a bigger vista than that, which is where the tank came into play. The ground floor of the prison was built on the floor of the tank, the ground floor of the film studio became the first floor of the prison, with cells positioned along the passageway, and then Tim built another floor on top of that, which could be walked on. It was a very clever design.'

One of the first sequences Sydney recalls filming on the new structure was the opening titles, which evocatively captured the sounds associated with prison life. 'After visiting various prisons as part of his research, Dick Clement told me that you constantly hear the jingling of keys and shutting of doors. This triggered me into thinking that perhaps we could use these sounds in the titles, thereby setting the scene for the programme. Prior to this, the opening-titles sequence for comedy programmes consisted mainly of music and graphics, but I didn't think that was the right style for *Porridge*, so took a different approach. To be honest, when I shot the titles at Ealing I was concerned people wouldn't like the end result. But everything turned out fine.'

People did like the style adopted for the opening credits. In *The Times* on 6 September 1974, Stanley Reynolds remarked how the title sequence 'seemed grim as an old Warner Brothers prison movie, with only the exaggerated military swagger of Fulton Mackay as the bantam-cock prison officer giving the comic game away'.

When a programme is recorded in front of an audience, the designer faces extra challenges. *Porridge* was no exception to this rule, as Tim explains. 'The audience takes up half the studio, leaving little space for artistic development. You have to try and turn the sets to face the audience, but, with all the cameras and equipment, some people haven't a clear view of what's going on and end up watching on the monitors fixed round the studio. But anything with Ronnie Barker in it will always be great, and I enjoyed the show immensely.'

Designing the Costumes by Mary Husband

In 1972 I designed the costumes for *The Two Ronnies* and my happy and artistically fulfilling period working with Ronnie Barker began – and it continued for the next fifteen years. We had previously met on *Before the Fringe*, directed by Robin Nash and introduced by Alan Melville. *The Two Ronnies* was something different: wittier than *Morecambe and Wise*, colourful and musical. And with scope for me: for period-costume design and the opportunity to design for dancers, such as Pan's People.

After my first series with the Ronnies, I set up costumes for *Open All Hours*, also directed by Sydney Lotterby – with whom I'd worked on *The Liver Birds* – so it was no surprise when I was asked to do the costumes for *Porridge*.

I didn't feel that being sent to jail was a lot of fun, so decided not to use the dark-navy prison uniforms. I thought that on the small screen they would be far too dark, en masse, and too similar to the prison officers' uniforms. I decided instead to dress the prisoners in grey battle-dress-style uniforms with the standard striped shirt. Having seen the film version recently on television, for which the designer used the navy uniforms, I think I made the right decision.

I went into fittings with Ronnie Barker, Brian Glover, Richard Beckinsale, Peter Vaughan, Tony Osoba, Sam Kelly, Ken Jones and an exciting cast of regular artistes. Fulton Mackay was an added joy: a sharp and brilliant performance as the chief prison officer. He wanted a flat, guards' cap with an officers' peak, which I altered specially, and the boots had to be perfect. Brian Wilde was the foil to Fulton: homely, laconic and a joy to work with.

Filming, though lots of fun, was very busy. Derek Sumner, an ex-actor (who in retirement returned to acting), was Ronnie's favourite dresser and my right-hand man. We filmed at both Ealing Studios, in Tim Gleeson's remarkable set, and at a psychiatric hospital that looked like an old Victorian prison, where we were met daily by fascinated inmates.

To help me bring reality and authenticity to my costumes I had the help of an advisor, Jonathan Marshall, a charmer who had done a spell of 'porridge' himself and written a book about his experiences. He told me all about boots, nightwear, arm bands for trusties and generally helped me pull the whole picture together. Working on *Porridge* was a joy.

Out in the Open Air

Although *Porridge* was largely shot in studios at Ealing and Television Centre, locations were occasionally sought for outdoor shots – such as that of the large, intimidating gates of Slade Prison shown during the opening titles. The responsibility for hunting down suitable locations for the programme was given to Ray Butt, the production assistant on series one. Ray, who retired from the BBC in 1987, after completing thirty-two years' service, had worked with

Sydney since the days of *The Liver Birds*, but their relationship dates back to 1956 when he joined the Beeb. 'Sydney used to be a cameraman, and when I joined as a kid at the bottom of the crew he was not only senior cameraman but also my boss. So, over the years, we've got to know each other well.'

As Sydney Lotterby points out, Ray's job wasn't an easy one. 'The prison authorities weren't very helpful. They wouldn't let us film anywhere, even *outside* a prison. And, although Dick Clement and Ian La Frenais were allowed in while they were conducting their research, neither the designer nor myself were allowed to look around.'

Being refused permission to film outside a real prison posed problems for Sydney and Ray, but the solution came in the shape of numerous psychiatric hospitals dotted around the London area. Ray retraces the steps he took in finding suitable locations. 'It was disappointing the Home Office refused us permission; if we'd been making a documentary or drama they might have considered our application, but not for a comedy. The institutions we found made suitable alternatives. We started at a grim-looking place

Fletch became a father figure to the naïve first-time offender Lennie Godber

near Watford. It reminded me of a Victorian workhouse – a dreadful building.' With all the windows and walkways barred, it resembled a prison. 'We only wanted to use the building for long shots, so it worked fine.' In fact, the selected location was so convincing that some viewers wrote to the production office asking which prison had been used.

Ray also found the gatehouse represented so effectively in the opening credits. Once marking the entrance to St Albans' Prison, the building became a military-detention barracks in 1915. A ten-year spell of non-occupancy followed before the local council acquired it and turned it into a depot for their highways department. Today, the building is used as a sales and marketing HQ for a leading mineral-water company.

No one would have guessed that behind those giant gates stood rows of dustcarts because, thanks to a few props – such as the prison nameplate and the barring of nearby windows – HMP Slade was born. 'Tim Gleeson made the exterior look as good as it did; but it was great finding the site with its authentic prison gates, even though they hadn't been used for some time,' says Ray.

The rest of the filming for the opening sequence then had to be organised, as Ray explains. 'We used some stock shots of doors closing, while the close-ups of hands turning keys were taken at cells in Shepherd's Bush police station. For timing purposes, we still needed a couple more shots, so I nipped down with a cameraman to the police station, where I'd established a few contacts since filming episodes of *Dixon of Dock Green* around there.' The opening-titles sequence was altered later in the series, showing Fletcher walking about the prison.

When he was assigned to the production team for *Porridge*, Ray was among those with initial reservations about the show's chances of longevity. However, his worries rapidly dispersed when the scripts arrived. 'I couldn't see how the idea could be developed for a whole series, but when I saw the scripts everything became clear. The laughs were cleverly written and had depth, while the characters were solid, three-dimensional figures.'

The production team was presented with a further headache at the start of the third series, when permission to film at the psychiatric hospital was withdrawn after complaints were received from those hospital visitors who were unhappy about the building representing a prison on TV. When scripts arrived, one of the jobs allocated to the production manager was to work through them and identify what scenes would be recorded using an outside location. Thus the incumbent Mike Crisp set about finding a new venue.

'When the hospital used in the first two series became unavailable, I looked around and found an institution in Ealing, which was ideal because it was near BBC's filming unit,' says Mike. The next step was to visit the establishment. 'The official showing me around suggested filming by a laundry block; he then took me to the hospital's Victorian square, which looked grim. I knew that it was going to be a fairly easy job for someone of Tim Gleeson's talent to make it resemble a prison, especially once he'd put a few fake bars up at the windows.'

While touring the establishment, Mike noticed that both the post box and telephone kiosk were painted blue. Curiosity soon got the better of him. 'I found it slightly odd, so asked if it was because we were on government property. The official giving me the guided tour replied: "Oh, no. One of our inmates has a particular problem whereby he puts litter in anything painted red. We had no choice but to paint them a different colour."'

Production secretary Judy Loe also remembers filming at the psychiatric institutes, but there is one particular moment that sticks in her mind. 'We were completing a scene where Lennie Godber was fighting while Fletcher and some other characters walked towards the scuffle; during the action, one of the hospital inmates threw urine at the actors! I couldn't believe it!'

Rehearsals and Recordings

Porridge – like many other BBC sitcoms – was recorded in front of a live audience. This would take place on Sundays at Television Centre, after a week of rehearsing. Any location filming required was completed prior to rehearsals. As soon as the scripts arrived, scenes necessitating outside shots or the use of the tank at Ealing Studios were identified. Usually a two-week period was set aside to shoot, edit and dub the filmed sequences prior to the relevant studio recording, during which they were shown to the audience.

The weekly timetable was tight, as Sydney explains. 'After Sunday's recording, Monday was a day off – before rehearsals started again on Tuesday. We'd rehearse right through until Saturday morning, after which we'd all go home for lunch. If the actors hadn't got it right by then, they never would.'

Series writers Clement and La Frenais were usually present during the read-throughs, a crucial stage in the production cycle. Ian elaborates: 'The read-through tells you a lot about how the script will work, although you usually come away with some rewrites. We'd normally return on the Thursday for the technical run, when a few more adjustments might be made.'

The quality of the scripts was such that extensive rewriting was unheard of. 'It seemed such an effortless process,' recalls Ian. 'During the third series, we were in America and missed quite a few of the read-throughs. Occasionally we'd carry out rewrites over the phone, but the scripts didn't change much.' While they were busy in the States, they relied heavily on Ronnie Barker's instincts. 'He was so good, and provided plenty of great one-liners, but it was awful being so far away and not part of the production. But we had little choice because by then we were starting to write the American version, *On the Rocks*. It was a busy time.'

Tony Osoba, who played McLaren, enjoyed everything about *Porridge*, even attending rehearsals. A milieu was created that was conducive to making a successful show. 'I looked forward to being with everyone, not just the cast but the whole production team, too,' says Tony. 'It was a positive experience, less troubled than some jobs I've been involved with. Often at rehearsals there's huge anxiety, and there can be tantrums, too. But there was none of that on *Porridge*; everything ran smoothly – we just got together, had a good time and the show seemed to have a natural momentum.'

During recording, Fulton Mackay's drive for perfection often led to retakes – something that frustrated Mike Crisp when he took over as production manager for the 1975 Christmas Special, 'The Desperate Hours', and series three. 'There's one shot I recall where Fulton comes into frame, adjusts his hat, pulls his trademark neck movement, then walks off. I lost count of the takes we did for that. It drove me up the wall because one of the production manager's responsibilities is the budget, and all these takes were costing us money.'

Sydney Lotterby remembers other such occasions involving Fulton. 'Fulton had to get his moves right. I remember one scene he walked into a cell and couldn't get his feet positioned right. He'd often walk into the cell on the wrong foot and say: "Sorry, I've done this wrong, can I start again?" Sometimes it became a bit wearing, especially after five or six takes, but the end result was always fine.'

But Mike, who left the BBC in 1996, admits he was never happy as a production manager, and saw it as a stepping-stone to becoming a director – a role he later held for many years. 'As production manager, you're pulling the whole project together, and if anything goes wrong, it's inevitably your fault!' he says, smiling. 'Somebody said to me once: "You're a lucky devil, aren't you? Whenever you do shows there's never any panic, nor rows – you must have a guardian angel." I felt like saying, "Don't you realise I work bloody hard?" To ensure everything ran smoothly, I always arrived an hour before anyone else just to think about what could possibly create chaos, thereby allowing me the chance to sort it out before anything blew up.'

Some actors find recording in front of a live audience unsettling – Ronnie Barker is not among them. 'The adrenaline flows when you have an audience in the studio,' he says. 'It always seemed like the scenes recorded in front of the audience got plenty of laughs, whereas the audience's reaction and laughter subsided when they watched the filmed sequences via the monitors in the studio. In my view, the audience is very important.'

Ronnie's vast experience in the profession has taught him that tension often exists in the television studio, and he has a method for smoothing the atmosphere, as Mike Crisp explains. 'A sitcom recording is about the most uncomfortable experience anybody could ever have. Not only are the seats excruciatingly uncomfortable, but also half a ton of hardware comes between you and what you want to see. Barker realised that tension in an audience would stop them laughing so used a regular ploy to relax everyone. Within the first few minutes, he'd deliberately dry, make a cock-up or blow a raspberry, which meant the scene had to be recorded again. He'd remark that it was his fault, then proceeded to play it as straight as he could, by which time the audience had relaxed.'

Among those watching the recordings were Dick Clement and Ian La Frenais. 'They were always great fun,' recalls Dick. 'Ronnie often did the warm-ups, which I don't think he enjoyed too much, and if there was a recording stop for any reason, he would always talk to the audience and keep them happy.

'Writing a series about prison is a hard sell, but with Ronnie Barker in the lead it immediately made it easy – because the moment he walked on the screen, there was an air of reassurance and you knew the show was going to be funny. He totally diffused any initial worries I had about the subject matter, and played a huge part in the show's success.'

Looking back, Sydney Lotterby has nothing but fond memories of making *Porridge*. These include the time Fulton Mackay was covered in soot while recording the episode 'The Hustler'. 'In the episode, Fletch and a few of the prisoners sneak into the boiler room to gamble on a game of snakes and ladders,' Sydney recalls. 'When Mackay finds out, he arranges for a delivery of coal to be poured through a hole into the boiler room. The next scene saw Ronnie and the others rushing out of the door.

'I started filming and noticed there wasn't any soot coming out of the door. So I asked the special effects man if he could make it more visible. He agreed. However, the worst thing you can say to an effects man is: "Can you do it a bit more?" This time the door opened and a great cloud of soot poured out. Brian Wilde and Fulton were standing against the wall opposite; when they moved, a soot outline was left behind. Fulton had soot in his ears for ages!'

Making-up

In terms of preparing actors for the recording of an episode, the genre of situation comedy invariably poses fewer problems for the make-up designer than other types of programme do. Make-up artist Ann Ailes-Stevenson spent twenty-seven years with the Beeb before going freelance, and during

It took over an hour to apply David Jason's make-up whenever he appeared as old man Blanco

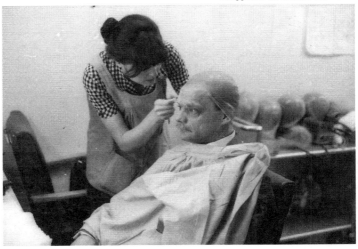

the 1960s and 1970s worked on plenty of comedies before concentrating mainly on period dramas. She was in charge of make-up for the second series of *Porridge*, and the biggest challenge she faced involved David Jason. She explains. 'David played Blanco, and we had to make him look old – something we achieved with the help of latex, which was stippled on. In those days it wasn't so sophisticated as it is now, because you didn't have so many latex pieces pre-made; you did everything on the day. And, to create the signs of ageing, you'd pinch the latex, forming creases.

'We then put a cap on his head, together with a fine wig, which allowed you to see bald patches. It took about an hour and a half every time we prepared him.'

Ronnie Barker's needs stretched to hair colouring. 'His natural colour is white, so we used a brown and reddish spray. It took about twenty minutes, because you had to be careful you didn't spray his scalp – getting the roots coloured entailed applying the spray with a toothbrush. Luckily, the spray didn't run under the heat of the lights, but it ran quite a lot when you applied it so you were always armed with a supply of cotton wool.'

Ann says that during her career she's enjoyed working on every show she's done. And it seems *Porridge* was no exception: 'There wasn't any difficulty with *Porridge*; everybody got on well together and it was like a big family.'

Making its Small-Screen Debut

The first series of *Porridge* kicked off with 'New Faces, Old Hands' on 5 September 1974. The episode centred on the arrival of three prisoners at Slade Prison: Fletcher, Godber and a simpleton called Heslop. The following day, Dick Clement was shooting a commercial and overheard the crew discussing the sitcom. 'No one realised I was involved in the series,' he says, 'so when they started talking about *Porridge*, my ears began flapping. It was very interesting because I got an immediate sense that the show had made a connection; the episode had been a hit and here was instant feedback –

it's hard to create that kind of buzz these days.'

Including the two Christmas Specials, a further nineteen episodes followed. Often, sitcoms can't sustain their momentum and tail off in terms of quality towards the end of their run, but this was not the case with *Porridge*. The quality remained high throughout, as acknowledged by Dick Clement – although he's the first to admit that some episodes were weaker than others. 'I felt happy with the standard of writing, and the second series was probably the best. During the first series we were feeling our way a bit, and there were a couple of episodes that didn't quite reach the level we wanted (an example of this is the episode 'A Day Out'). But by the second series, the plots were much tighter and we began writing for the strengths we'd identified within the show.'

One of the beauties of Clement and La Frenais' writing is their propensity for mixing a fair dosage of realism into comedic scripts, as exemplified masterfully by the first-series episode 'A Night In'. Behind the funny situations and humorous lines lies a resonance usually reserved for more serious studies of social and human behaviour. Fearful of his first night inside, Godber is shown the key to survival by the ripened criminal Fletcher, who quickly adopts parental-like feelings towards the young inmate sharing his cell. 'It was important we studied such issues,' says Dick. 'In a way, this episode gave us a focus for the series. The relationship between Fletcher and Godber became a kind of mentor-protégé situation; that scenario developed organically, we didn't sit down and plan it like that.'

Dick Clement admits that Galton and Simpson's writing influenced both Ian and him. 'We always wanted our scripts to have depth, just like Galton and Simpson's *Steptoe*. In that series, there's a real sense of sadness and frustration, which became something of a trend at the time. Without doubt, the best situation comedy has something more going for it; we wanted that as part of our work, too.'

By the time the third series had been commissioned, Dick and Ian were living in America, from where the scripts were written. Inevitably, their presence was missed on the set, but the writers believe the series still contained some good material. Their confidence – not only in their own writing but also in the capabilities of the team they'd left behind – was high. Dick and Ian were happy for alterations to be made to their scripts, although the necessity for such was remarkably rare. Jimmy Gilbert recalls the respect they held for Ronnie Barker. 'They knew he was a good writer and, as they were back and forth to America, they had total confidence in Ronnie's good faith and judgement, knowing he wouldn't change something for the sake of it. So, if I had problems getting hold of them, I knew they were happy if Ronnie, for example, wanted to make tiny changes to ensure a particular line was more comfortable for him.'

Jimmy Gilbert felt the sitcom scored top marks in all aspects, including the style of recording. 'Although it was shot in front of an audience, Syd Lotterby always did fourth-wall shots at the end, as pick-up shots. Normally you wouldn't be able to do that, because one wall of a room or set has to be kept open because the audience and cameras are all out front facing in. But Syd wanted the fourth-wall shot, to add that extra bit of reality.'

Sydney Lotterby explains: 'I got tired of always facing the same way in the cell, so I asked Tim Gleeson to paint a cloth that could be used to extend the cell. But as soon as someone opened a door on the stage the whole cloth moved, making it look as if the back of the cell was moving. We soon put a stop to that and found it gave the set some depth.'

Where Did You Get That Name?

Dick Clement and Ian La Frenais have a propensity for using old friends' names for their fictional characters, a trait first seen in *The Likely Lads* and used in most of their work since. *Porridge* was no exception, with Godber's namesake being a London-based hairdresser who cut Dick and Ian's hair from his salon. 'My name is Denny Godber, and my junior at that time was Lennie, so I think Dick and Ian

swapped the names around and came up with Lennie
Godber.'

Denny sold his salon fifteen years ago, but still cuts Dick
and Ian's hair, as well as Jenny Clement's, Dick's ex-wife.
'Whenever the boys are over from America, they'll always
visit my home, where I have a new salon in the basement.'

Born in Cornwall, Denny attended art school in Plymouth
before leaving the Southwest for the bright lights of London.
After retraining, he found work at Sweeney's, one of the first
male hairdressing salons in the capital, whose clientele
included rock stars and actors. Denny, who's now fifty-four,
was initially employed as a junior but by 1975 had bought
the salon. He later took a year off and toured with various
pop stars – including Rod Stewart, Queen and Led Zeppelin
– in his capacity as a hairdresser.

Origins of 'Porridge'

The derivation of the term 'porridge' is uncertain, but
Bloomsbury's *Euphemisms* states that the word may have
been inspired by 'stodgy prison food, which has to be stirred
. . . an allusion to the slang *stir*, which means prison'. It's
thought that the term dates back to the 1830s.

Meanwhile, Rannoch Daly, who was Assistant Governor
at Chelmsford Prison when the *Porridge* movie was made,
explains: 'By tradition, if a prisoner does not finish eating all
his porridge for breakfast on his last day in prison he'll have
to return to finish it later. Thus the phrase "doing porridge"
applies to second and subsequent periods of imprisonment
and is particularly appropriate to the old lag Norman Stanley
Fletcher.'

Reviewing the Success

With more than sixteen million people tuning in to watch the
opening instalment, *Porridge* became an instant hit. While
evaluating a show's success isn't the easiest of tasks – why
one show clicks and another flops defies logic at times – it

was fairly obvious why Clement and La Frenais' slice of prison life was so readily accepted. 'Not only did they deliver brilliant scripts – it was also arguably Ronnie Barker's best-ever performance; he was wonderful,' enthuses Jimmy Gilbert.

'If you think about the ingredients of a successful situation comedy, it's clear the characters must be more than just life-like: they also have to be interdependent, rather like *Steptoe and Son*, where the two of them can't live with each other but couldn't survive without the other. They were locked into a situation, and it never worked so well when Galton and Simpson sent them on holiday, or put them into a different environment.

'With *Porridge*, the characters also found themselves locked into their own little world. And there were threats all around: from fellow prisoners, from the screws and the system. All these elements added the tension that situation comedy requires.'

The media's reviewers were almost unanimous in their adulation for Clement and La Frenais' masterpiece. In his aforementioned *Times* article of September 1974, Stanley Reynolds wrote: 'How quickly *Porridge* . . . established the main characters, the comic situation, and its style of play in its first half-hour.' Clive James commented in the *Observer*, 'Those scripts by Clement and La Frenais were good in every molecule.'

The *Guardian*, meanwhile, carried an article by Peter Fiddick, who commented that it would require a 'great deal of ingenuity' to make the series work. 'Setting a comedy series in a prison imposes restrictions that seem to close visibly like an Edgar Allan Poe cell the more you think of them.' But he was nonetheless impressed by what he saw of the new sitcom: 'Clement and La Frenais seem to have absorbed something about prisons and their constraints, on which to build. It could be a new source of comedy.'

When asked to nominate his favourite episodes, Ronnie Barker cites 'A Night In' as one of which he's particularly fond. 'Syd's idea of building a second set of the cell to obtain an all-round feel meant we could cut between the two; it worked well and gave a claustrophobic feel to the episode. You never felt disappointed with any of the scripts, and another one that was good fun was "A Day Out". But I think more humour came from the concentrated situations inside the jail.'

'A Night In' is also one of Ian's favourite episodes, though he has a few regrets about the first series. 'Although there were a couple of great episodes, it was the weakest series. Dick and I felt we couldn't write the series without an episode showing what it's really like being locked away. "A Night In" really holds up, but there are one or two others that are too broad, such as "A Day Out". This was probably because we were still finding our way with the tone of the show, whereas by the second and third series the episodes were very solid.'

As for Dick, he's also keen on 'A Night In', as well as 'The Harder They Fall' and 'Just Desserts'. 'I'm very fond of that one because it's a whole episode about one tiny thing. In a way, that was the key to the series: picking something minute and constructing an episode around it.'

While Dick and Ian had initially worried about the plots, they eventually realised that the show was so character-driven they could rely on the simplest of storylines. (One episode, 'Just Desserts', for example, revolved around the disappearance of a can of pineapple.) 'As the series progressed, we built up the confidence to focus on much simpler themes, whereas previously some of the plots and storylines were too convoluted, resulting in the episodes being broader than they merited,' says Ian La Frenais.

As far as Sydney Lotterby is concerned, 'Just Desserts' and 'The Harder They Fall' are his favourite episodes from a sitcom he regards as among the best he's produced. 'It's a toss-up between *Porridge; Yes, Minister* and *Yes, Prime Minister*, but Clement and La Frenais' work was excellent.'

For least favoured episodes, Sydney points to 'No Peace For the Wicked', from series two, while Dick Clement didn't enjoy 'A Day Out'. 'It was the weakest in series one. We thought we needed a breath of fresh air, to get out of prison once in a while, but as soon as we had recorded it we realised it was best to stick with the limitations of the prison setting. In hindsight, I think we'd written "A Day Out" out of panic, thinking we couldn't possibly write six episodes based entirely in prison – but, of course, we could.'

With regular airings on terrestrial and satellite television, and the recent release of a boxed set of videos containing every episode, *Porridge* lives on – not that Jimmy Gilbert is surprised. 'There are few comedies that don't date; you even have to be careful with many of the classics now if you're selecting something for a repeat run, but crime and punishment are universal themes that won't date – which is great news for *Porridge* fans.'

Dick is occasionally asked by friends to show an episode of the sitcom. 'I'm very proud of the series and think it holds up well, even after all these years. It still makes me laugh and I never tire of watching it; in fact, I could sit down and watch most of the episodes any time.

'The show got off to a flying start. There was so much interest in it; I remember doing lots of interviews before the series came out, and felt it was going to attract a big audience. Fortunately, most people stuck with it. There had been an enormous amount of anticipation because of Ronnie Barker appearing in a prison series written by us. The main elements in the show appealed to people, including the idea of the guys bucking the system against all the odds, and, with the tremendous chemistry between everyone, it had plenty going for it. Unlike the success of some of our other shows, *Porridge*'s popularity didn't really take us by surprise.'

As for its continued success on British screens, Dick says: 'Its theme is pretty timeless; prison hasn't changed much, and the thought of people trying to survive and make the best of a bad situation is appreciated by all.'

Mike Crisp feels much of the credit for the show's success lies with Barker and Beckinsale. 'They got on so well professionally and never rowed. But, of course, there were other factors, including the quality of the scripts and the writers choosing an absolutely classic situation. Comedy comes from friction, which is in plentiful supply when people from all walks of life are trapped together – and you can't get anymore trapped than prison.'

Director Sydney Lotterby, meanwhile, believes one of the show's greatest strengths is its believability, even though it's outside the sphere of most people's experience. 'The characters are accepted as truthful, and the situation regarded as fairly representative of prison life. You have to suspend belief in any comedy, but most of the better sitcoms are realistic.'

In hindsight, there's little Sydney would change if he were making *Porridge* today. 'When Fletcher and Godber are in their cell there's hardly any noise in the background and now I'm disappointed with that aspect. At the time it was felt background noise would be a distraction; it's a shame I didn't do something because there's always noise in prison. But that's the only thing I would do differently.'

Dick Clement has little he'd alter second time around. 'I would have used Fulton more, particularly in the early days when I felt we were a bit profligate with Mackay.' He would also have ensured every episode unfolded within the confines of the prison walls. 'I wouldn't have gone outside like we did with "A Day Out"; it was better keeping the characters contained.'

Making Music

Given the job of writing the music for the theme tune, with lyrics sung by Ronnie Barker himself, was Max Harris, who'd worked with Jimmy Gilbert on numerous television productions. Max was commissioned to write the signature tunes for other pilots within the *Seven of One* series, including 'Open All Hours'.

Max, whose tune is mainly heard with the closing titles, wasn't briefed on what was expected; he was simply sent the script and it was left to his discretion what he came up with.

'In "Prisoner and Escort" the main character – Fletcher –

was a Cockney character, so, when it came to writing the signature tune, I felt it needed a Cockney tune – most of which are associated with music-hall themes. So that's the kind of sound which eventually evolved,' says Max, who has written more than fifty signature tunes for television programmes, including *Mind Your Language, Doomwatch, Sherlock Holmes* and *The Strange World of Gurney Slade*.

After kicking ideas around in his brain for some time, it took Max only a couple of hours to actually write the composition; then followed a three-hour session in the studio. He still gets pleasure from hearing his theme tune whenever *Porridge* is repeated. 'And I still collect some royalties, which is nice – it keeps my bank manager a bit happier, I suppose!'

Bringing Down the Curtain on Slade Prison

Ronnie Barker's wish to move on to pastures new was the fundamental reason that the third series of life at Slade was the last. Sydney Lotterby admits that everyone was sad when the closing episode, 'Final Stretch', was complete, but also knew there was no chance of a further series. 'You don't persuade Ronnie; he's a very strong character. Once he'd made up his mind that he didn't want to do any more, there was no going back. It was disappointing, but there were new projects to move on to.'

Dick Clement and Ian La Frenais would willingly have written a further series of *Porridge*, as Ian explains. 'We ended with a kind of compromise by doing *Going Straight*. We just felt we couldn't abandon the character – people still wanted to see him. I think *Porridge* would have taken another series, but Ronnie is a prolific entertainer and had lots on his plate; he was always working and wanted to move on.' Ian didn't try changing Ronnie's mind. 'We all agreed in the end, although Dick and I knew we could do something else with it after a little pause. Then, of course, Lew Grade had told us he wanted to make a feature film of it, so we also had that to write.'

'I'm sure we could have written another series,' adds Dick, 'but on reflection we felt we'd just about done it all. I wasn't particularly disappointed – I didn't think of it in those terms. It was time to move on and I thought of the series with nothing but pleasure, because it really was totally painless.'

It's now more than thirty years since the pilot episode was first transmitted, and the series is still going strong. A year doesn't go by without *Porridge* repeats being shown by the BBC and the satellite station UK Gold. No one seems to tire of Fletcher and co., and the series always attracts glowing reviews whenever it's shown. Writing for the *Western Mail* back in July 1984, journalist Gethyn Stoodley Thomas remarked how 'far ahead of any new comedy series' it was, while Garry Bushell said in the *Sun* in 1990: 'Aren't those *Porridge* repeats the business? Ronnie Barker's wily old lag Fletcher is a classic comedy creation and the scripts are a joy.' And even in 1992 the show was still warmly received. So impressed was Richard Last by the series that he wrote in an article in the *Daily Telegraph*: 'Sometimes I wonder if the BBC is doing itself any favours by re-transmitting this eighteen-year-old series. It is so perfectly scripted, so beautifully acted, so full of humanity and so stomach-clutchingly funny, that it makes almost every contemporary TV comedy look wan.'

Without doubt, *Porridge* has become one of the elite in the sitcom genre, a ratings-winner that can be relied upon to hold its own against its more up-front, brash, younger siblings. Journalist Hilary Doling, writing in the *Sunday Express* back in 1984, summed up beautifully the calibre of the show when she said: 'It must be the only porridge that gets better with age.' How right she is.

THE WRITERS

Dick Clement

Even as a young boy, Dick Clement aspired to making people laugh. The youngest of five children, he admired his elder brother's ability to have the rest of the family in stitches. 'I saw how much Arthur got away with and knew I wanted to emulate him. I've always liked the feeling of making people laugh; when the family did laugh for the first time in response to one of my jokes, it was very satisfying,' recalls Dick, who tried his hand at writing from an early age.

His attempt to pen a radio show fell short of requirements, but the seed had been sown for what would become a glittering career. 'I was about eight when I tried writing an episode for the *Paul Temple* series, except it only lasted three minutes instead of thirty!'

When it dawned on Dick that he'd have to make a living, writing didn't seem a viable option. It was only later, while working for the BBC, that he rekindled his interest in writing. 'It's strange that it was only then that I remembered this foreshadowing that I had tried writing at a young age – I'd forgotten all about it.'

Born in Westcliff-on-Sea in Essex in 1937, Dick savoured a happy childhood on the coast. 'One of the things Ian and I have in common is that we both grew up in seaside towns: Ian in Whitley Bay, me in Westcliff. It was fun having the sea nearby. I remember the immediate post-war years, when mines were slowly being removed from the beaches and I explored bombed-out houses with other kids.'

Dick's father ran a successful milk business that employed his two brothers, but Dick was determined to pursue a different path. Although keen on writing, Dick's early ambition was to become an actor. 'The most important thing I did at school was act in school plays – I took it very seriously. I'm not sure if I would have made a very good actor, but the exposure was valuable later when I began directing and writing. There's an enormous overlap between the skills of acting and directing or producing; so the more experienced you are, the better you'll understand the business as a whole.'

Someone who encountered Dick's bent for acting is his old school-friend Terry Taylor. They met at Bishop's Stortford College, while in their early teens. 'Dick was in the dramatic society, and we were both in a puppet club as well,' says Terry. With the help of rudimentary tape recorders they visited local schools. 'We'd use string puppets, and Dick was always good with the voices on the recorder.

'Culturally, he was a big influence on me. He was always first into things, like Hemingway and other authors of the day. Once he asked whether I listened to *The Goon Show*. I didn't, but made sure I did the following week. We'd then imitate all the voices.' Terry also recalls putting their Saturday-morning study periods to good use. 'We'd creep off and listen to the repeat; it was a joy hearing it all over again. Dick was a boarder and I was a day-boy – I don't know how we chummed up. I think we used to laugh at each other's jokes and consequently became good friends.'

After leaving school, Terry worked in accountancy while Dick crossed the Atlantic on an exchange visit with an American school. He values those twelve months spent in the States. 'It's one of the most important things that has happened to me,' he says. 'During my sixth-form year, I became friends with an American who was on an exchange deal. I kept thinking how fantastic it must be to spend a year at school in a different country, learning about a completely new culture.'

After mulling over the opportunity, Dick applied for a place on the exchange scheme and was accepted. 'I'm proud I had the nous to go for it. Selection was based on an inter-view, and I'm reasonably good at talking, so felt confident about securing one of the eighteen spaces available to thirty-five applicants.'

Dick sailed to the States in 1955 on the *Queen Mary* and returned on the *Queen Elizabeth* a year later, having experienced in America a rehearsal for where life would eventually lead him. 'It was a real love affair, I had a wonderful time,' he enthuses. 'We were like ambassadors in many ways, so we had to behave, but I found the work very easy and felt it was a fantastic experience.' Dick believes the confidence he gained stood him in good stead for completing his national service upon returning. 'It helped me bullshit my way into a commission, separating me from the herd,' he says. 'It was a very important experience for an eighteen-year-old.'

Joining the RAF, Dick was stationed in Norfolk. Based at the same training camp at Bircham Newton was Michael Burridge, who played a key role in Dick's life after demob: not only did he play a part in introducing Dick to Ian La Frenais, but also helped with his search for employment. 'After we'd finished national service, I noticed in a newspaper advert that the BBC were looking for studio managers. I sent it to Dick, suggesting he apply – which, of course, he did.'

Michael's not surprised Dick has become one of the country's greatest comedy writers, having experienced his wit first hand. 'He was always very funny; the humour of life never escaped him. The way his career has turned out is no surprise to me.'

Back on civvy street, Dick knew it was time to establish a footing in the working world. After considering applying for RADA, he decided instead to respond to the BBC's advert for studio managers, and was successful in his application. 'I still wasn't entirely sure what I really wanted to do with my life, but joined the Corporation because I felt in the vaguest possible way that it was the right direction for me.'

Dick started his media career as a studio manager, or what he terms a 'glorified sound-man'. After training, he joined Bush House, where broadcasts were transmitted all over the world. 'It was very interesting at first and, although the work got boring after a while, the people were great. Most of the time you were putting out new broadcasts, perhaps in Albanian or Polish, and you couldn't understand a word.'

His subsequent transfer to the African Service afforded him the chance to complete his first piece of professional writing. 'I wrote a script in English, which was translated into Somali: that's the first time I put words on paper in a specialist capacity.'

While working for the BBC, Dick started writing for pleasure, contributing sketches and ideas to the Corporation's own drama group, the Ariel Players. His involvement with the Players grew as he began using the revues as a vehicle for developing his writing of comedy and satire. His association with the group was memorable in other ways: it was during the after-show party of the 1961 performance that Dick met his first wife. Jenny had played no part in the performance, but was invited along by Brenda Punshon (née Shepherd), who'd appeared in seven of the sketches and arranged the dance numbers for the Christmas show. 'I shared a flat with Jenny, while Dick shared a flat with Terry Taylor, who I went out with for a while,' she says.

The party was held at Dick's flat in Earls Court, and Brenda recalls introducing them to each other. 'That was the end of Jenny for me!' laughs Brenda. 'We'd planned to go to America together the following year, but she pulled out and ended up marrying Dick instead. I was still in the States at the time, much to my annoyance, but I managed to phone them at the wedding from San Francisco.' Jenny later returned the compliment by introducing Brenda to her husband, Richard.

Jenny remembers hitting it off with Dick immediately, partly because of their penchant for a little bear! 'We both adore Winnie-the-Pooh,' she explains, 'and were able to quote huge sections from stories as well as reciting the poems to each other. I found Dick quite imposing when we first met, because he's very tall. But intellectually we hit it off from the start, and began dating straight away. We continued talking about Winnie-the-Pooh from that first meeting and, as you can imagine, our children were brought up on the bear as well.'

Back at the BBC, Dick's duties started to encompass magazine programmes, voice work and producing. After five years, however, he was ready for a change. 'I was desperate to get into mainstream broadcasting, I felt in an incredible backwater,' he says. To achieve his aim he was accepted on a BBC directors' course; this led to the filming of a sketch titled 'Double Date', on the strength of which Dick and Ian were commissioned to write their first television sitcom: *The Likely Lads*. Dick was still employed by the Beeb when the series started life, but left to pursue a career as a freelance scriptwriter as its success picked up momentum.

Nowadays Dick is based in the States, where he lives with his second wife, Nancy. When it comes to recreation, his main interest is playing tennis in the Californian sun. 'I play as often as I can, usually two or three games a week. It's good fun and ideal for keeping fit. It's also a great way to unwind, especially after a hard day's work.'

Ian La Frenais

Like so many teenagers on the verge of leaving school, Ian La Frenais didn't know what he wanted from life. His father was a corporate accountant, but Ian, an only child, knew that wasn't the career for him. 'I was interested in art, but also had a leaning towards writing – or wanting to write – but didn't know how to progress the idea,' he says. 'In addition to writing essays at school, I wrote for pleasure, so for a while I considered being a journalist.'

Mike Thompson – who's known Ian since junior school and grew up in an adjoining street in Whitley Bay – says Ian's ambition to write existed from a young age. 'At school he was good at English and always keen to get into writing, but I think he probably saw himself as a novelist rather than writing for television. One of his great talents is instant recall of situations and conversations he'd had, or overheard, stretching back to his childhood, which has made him a good raconteur.'

Fellow schoolmate Horace Jeffcock remembers Ian as a 'fun guy'. 'He was always imagining funny situations, trying to create an amusing scene out of something we were looking at or talking about. That sense of humour was built in to him.'

Ian's uncertainty about a future career extended beyond his school days. After leaving the Dame Allan's School he had a year to kill before university. It was during this period that he decided against higher education and to complete his national service in the army. 'Even then I'd tell people I was going to be a writer, but it was a lie because I didn't have any clear ideas about what I wanted to do – it just sounded a glamorous thing to say.'

Although he spent his national service at Blenheim Barracks, Aldershot, Ian regularly returned home, as old friend Vin Welch recalls. 'He managed to get a job in the office issuing passes, so ended up with an inordinate amount of weekend passes!' Vin remembers a time when Ian went AWOL. 'After coming back for a weekend, a few friends went to the station to see him off before going on to a party. Ian was so annoyed about missing the do that he decided not to return.' He went to the party with his friends and the following day visited his doctor, feigning illness, thus preventing trouble when he reached his army base.

Another of Ian's friends was David Hallwood, who attended Bygate Infant School at Monkseaton, and Park Primary in Whitley Bay with Ian. The pair joined up on the same day. 'We thought it best to get national service over and done with,' he says. 'Put on the London train by our folks in September 1955, neither of us had spent time away from home before; but we ended up laughing from dawn till dusk as Ian came to terms with the army. The "regular" NCOs couldn't get their brains round the name La Frenais so Ian was known as "Lee Francis" for the term of our square-bashing.

'Ian was constantly inventing characters in his imagination. One was a mild little creature who dribbled and kept looking up into the eyes of his corporal and did everything he was told to the letter! If he saw a railway-hoarding advising people to go to Margate for their summer holidays, then Ian's make-believe character was off to Kent.

'Another of his ruses was to get the whole platoon, when marching from one place to another, to stamp on every seventh step, causing drill corporals near seizures as they struggled to work out what was happening. Ian was liked by all the rookie soldiers, even though we were a mixed bunch – with university graduates, public-school-leavers, ordinary working-class lads and one or two thugs. We all mixed in together and produced a winning "B" Company in the drill competition at the end of ten weeks.'

After returning to civvy street, Ian moved between jobs before parental pressure forced a decision. 'For a while it felt as if my life was in limbo, and it was quite nice,' he admits. But his father had begun to urge him to make something of his life, so he joined the tobacco company Gallahers as a sales trainee and spent the next two years working throughout the British Isles. 'I spent a lot of my youth smoking free cigarettes!'

Ian's life reached a crucial juncture during 1961, when some of his friends ditched their jobs and moved to London. Brian Flint, who started off as a teacher before going into advertising, and Maurice Hardaker, a physicist, wanted to break into the world of entertainment themselves. While living in the Northeast, they had secured a weekly slot on Tyne Tees – the regional independent television station – performing a satirical song, as Maurice explains. 'While Brian wrote the words, I composed the music. We appeared every week for a couple of years, back in the late fifties. We enjoyed it so much, we moved to London to see if we could

make a career out of it. We'd already agreed that if we didn't
make a lot of money we'd pack it in and return to something
sensible.'

With another of his friends, Horace Jeffcock, already in
London, Ian started getting itchy feet for the capital's
bright lights. 'During that period, when economically
everything was going well, "Going to London" had a
certain significance,' Ian explains, 'and didn't beg the question: "What are you going to do when you get there?" It
was simply a state of mind, I had no idea what I was
going to do!'

So, having decided that his future lay south, Ian headed
for London, escorted by Mike Thompson. 'A friend and I
took him down as he went to start his career as the author
of the century!' smiles Mike. 'He had ambitions of being
interviewed by John Freeman on *Face to Face*, having written
his first novel.' Initially he lived with Maurice and Brian in
Earls Court before sharing a flat with Brian Flint in Pont
Street, Knightsbridge.

To earn some cash, Ian worked for a cleaning company
and had other jobs before joining Marketing Advisory
Service, a market-research company. He was recruited by
George Murray, who later set up his own company,
Marketing Economics, and invited Ian to join him. They
became good friends. 'Ian was always an amusing character,' says George, who was aware of his employee's
writing ambitions. 'He was working for me when *The
Likely Lads* first started. He has a very creative and distinctive talent, so I wasn't surprised when he eventually went
part-time, then gradually filtered out altogether to spend
more time writing.'

George enjoyed working with Ian. 'I wouldn't say he was
a born market-researcher, but he had a good analytical mind,
could do research and was able to write reports – I wouldn't
have employed him if he hadn't been competent.'

One thing George remembers clearly about Ian was his eye
for a fast car. 'When he was working for me, he demanded a
company car. I thought he was going to choose a Ford

Cortina or something, but he wanted our red Sunbeam Alpine. Later, when he had a bit more money he bought himself an E-type Jag, then a Rolls-Royce – he even had his own chauffeur for a while.'

Writer Patrick Tilley, who'd already written several episodes of the Rediffusion series *Crane* when he first met Ian, also recalls this passion for cars. 'When Ian and Dick's stardom was beginning to go into ascendancy, Ian came round to my house in Highgate and asked me to look out the window. There was this dark-blue E-type Jag; it was a real "bird-puller". He was absolutely thrilled with it, and had bought it on the strength of the money he'd received for one of *The Likely Lads* series.' Patrick asked whether his family was happy about his success. 'He replied: "Yes, but my mother told me not to give up the day job!"'

Eventually Ian – who's now married to Doris and has one stepson, Michael – decided it was time to quit market research and concentrate on writing full-time. 'Throughout the period Dick and I wrote the first two series of *The Likely Lads*, as well as our first screenplay, *The Jokers*, I continued working in market research. But I began feeling I was missing out on all the fun of recording the episodes – and when the BBC ordered a third series of *The Likely Lads*, it seemed the ideal moment to put "professional writer" on the passport!'

The Writing Partnership

There aren't many writing partnerships that have lasted as long as the one forged nearly four decades ago by Dick Clement and Ian La Frenais. When they started penning skits for the amateur productions of the BBC's Ariel Players, they had no idea their talents would take them to Hollywood. Without question, theirs is one of the most respected and sought-after teams in the entertainment business – as proven by their ever-increasing lists of credits and awards.

Since the mid-1970s, Dick and Ian have lived in Beverly Hills. 'We sort of explored the idea of moving here in 1974,' explains Ian. 'But it wasn't until the end of '75 that we actually moved. Even though we were based in the States, we were constantly working for the British market throughout the remainder of the seventies and early eighties, which meant commuting for some time. Even in 1979, when we formed a production company and had offices in America and England, nearly all the work was London-generated. Gradually the writers accepted that the States had become their home, and began to settle. 'As the years passed and I married an American, established more and more American friends, I began realising my future lay here,' Ian continues.

Initially, Dick and Ian moved to the States to be near the centre of the movie industry. Following the success of their early sitcoms, they branched out into writing film scripts, starting with *The Jokers* in 1967, then *Otley*, a year later, which Dick also directed, and *Hannibal Brooks*, telling the story of a POW escaping over the Alps with an elephant. With Hollywood being the hub of the movie world, living within close proximity seemed crucial for Clement and La Frenais' future. But it was the writers' track record in sitcoms that agents seized upon when they touched down on American soil, and it wasn't long before they were involved in negotiations concerning an American version of *Porridge*. *On the Rocks* was screened in 1976 but never progressed beyond the first series.

Neither Dick nor Ian would consider returning to England: they enjoy their lives in Beverly Hills too much. 'It's a hard-working town, very work orientated,' says Dick. 'We have a routine: Ian comes around at about nine-thirty each morning, and we work till four-thirty. He's better at dialogue, while I'm better at structure; so together we work well.

'I'm very happy being based here, but we'd never stop writing for Britain: we still find that writing with a British voice is easier than writing with an American one. We like showing we're flexible and capable of more than one style, but it's enormously comfortable writing with a British voice.'

Although they've written for the American market, it's

something they find difficult and not particularly gratifying. 'We haven't been very successful at it, apart from writing for *The Tracey Ullman Show*, which is great fun,' says Dick. 'But that's for cable, where you have a lot more freedom; in fact, it's the nearest we've come to the freedom we were given on British television.'

Dick claims that writing for network television in the States is a 'young man's game'. 'You also need a lot of stamina because it's not really a writer's medium, it's a producer's. But that's not to say all American TV isn't funny: the best American comedy is fantastic – and in many ways they're better at writing comedy than the British.'

Much of the duo's success is down to their deep under-standing of each other, something that has developed over the years. 'It's been an enormously long and successful working marriage,' says Dick. 'But we've also worked on our own: Ian has written *Lovejoy* and *Spender*, while I've directed movies and a stage play. The break always proves productive and refreshing, but we've never wanted to break up the part-nership. It's more fun writing a script together: you can prop each other up as well as make each other laugh.'

Although they've enjoyed many successes during their careers, Clement and La Frenais are unable to pick a favourite. 'I have great respect for *The Likely Lads* because it was the series that got us started, but I wouldn't put it ahead of *Porridge* or *Auf Wiedersehen, Pet* – they're equally impor-tant,' says Dick.

'You write shows at different periods of your career, so it's difficult pinpointing one in particular,' Ian agrees. 'I enjoyed writing *Porridge*, and it was definitely the hardest to pull off. But you continue to learn; I feel we're better writers now than we were three or four years ago, which means it's not easy picking the best work we've done.'

One person who can testify to the quality of scripts in *Porridge* is Ronnie Barker, who feels that Clement and La Frenais' work oozed quality. 'The wonderful thing was you just picked up the script and did it. It was complete and well rounded, everything was there; you never needed to add a word. I never thought, 'This line isn't good enough', or 'This sequence doesn't work', because it always did.

'Occasionally I would add the odd word if I felt it would make something work better. I rarely did that sort of thing on the recording night because it's very dangerous – but if things were going well I couldn't resist it sometimes,' smiles Ronnie. 'I remember there was a prison visitors' scene and I was sitting with Patricia Brake – who was playing Fletcher's daughter – and Fulton started making this strange noise, so I turned to Patricia and said, "He does bird impressions now", which got a laugh. But Dick and Ian's work was always spot-on.'

One of Clement and La Frenais' trademarks is the strength of their characters. Pick up any one of their scripts and you won't find a barrowful of gags. Instead, you will see a depth of character an actor can really get his teeth into. 'We're not gag writers,' says Ian, 'we obtain humour from the characters themselves.' You need look no further than *Porridge* and *The Likely Lads* for proof that this works: the situation in both sitcoms is harsh, but the colour of the characters cleverly balances the grimness.

Patrick Tilley co-wrote a number of sketches for the Ariel Players and, later, novelised several scripts for a BBC book based on *Whatever Happened to the Likely Lads?* He has known Dick and Ian for years, and admires their work. 'They're on the same wavelength, and have a certain magic between them. It's a unique collaboration and fascinating to watch.' And Patrick's been fortunate enough to do just that. 'While Ian was walking around, Dick was sprawled out on a chaise longue, scribbling everything down. They work directly on to a computer these days, but when I saw them, Ian would spark off things, perhaps snatches of dialogue, and Dick would organise it and write it all down. It was great to observe.'

Though it is success that we readily associate with Clement and La Frenais, they have also endured the odd disappointment. Not everything they touch turns to gold – their 1993 comedy-drama for ITV, *Full Stretch*, being a prime case in point. 'I really felt that would work,' says Ian, 'but the programme wasn't given a chance to settle, because there were changes taking place in ITV at the time. It was a shame because the casting was wonderful and we felt we had created the new *Minder*.'

That said, many writers would give anything to taste a little of the success Dick and Ian have experienced in the field of sitcoms. They won The Society of Film and Television Arts award for both *Whatever Happened to the Likely Lads?* and *Porridge*, as well as picking up a Screen Writers' Guild award for their prison-based series. And yet, despite the critical acclaim they've enjoyed with their classic contribution to the genre, Dick and Ian are in no rush to return to it. 'Situation comedy is not my favourite genre,' Dick admits. 'I like everything we do to contain comedy, but I don't really want to go back to that. I find the tyranny of having to be funny all the time exhausting. I like it when you can be both. It's still tremendously satisfying hearing people laugh at something you've written, but it's gratifying to occasionally write a scene where the audience go quiet and are touched by what they see. In a way, the juxtaposition of the two is the ideal.'

But whatever they write in the future, humour will always be an integral component. 'I'd never want to write something without humour,' says Dick, 'because I think it's essential. Even in the darkest, most heavy movie it's important because life contains humour – often in the most inappropriate places – and I like that.'

It seems that writing situation comedy is an enervating exercise and not to be taken lightly. 'It's great when you finish it, but, boy, it's hard work,' Dick explains. 'When you set out to be funny and people don't laugh, you've failed one hundred per cent. And you know it because you can hear the silence; whereas if you write a thriller and people are fairly thrilled, it's not such a dramatic failure. It's only comedy where you have this absolute situation: do they laugh or not. And when they don't, it's very, very painful.'

FILM CREDITS include

The Jokers   The Likely Lads   Villain   Otley

Porridge   The Prisoner of Zenda   Still Crazy

Hannibal Brooks

THEATRE

Billy   CREDITS include

Porridge sketch for
The Two Ronnies stage show

TV
CREDITS include

Whatever Happened to   Mog   Porridge

The Likely Lads   the Likely Lads?   Going Straight

Mr Aitch   The New Adventures
of Lucky Jim   Freddie and Max

The Further Adventures
of Lucky Jim   Seven of One ('Prisoner and Escort'
and 'I'll Fly You for a Quid')

Auf Wiedersehen, Pet   The Old Boy Network   The Highwayman

Full Stretch   The Tracey Ullman Show (US)

Over the Rainbow

Rita Moreno Show (US)   Billy Liar (pilot for US)

Thick as Thieves

On The Rocks (US)

Dick also directed the second series of Not Only . . . But Also in 1966, as
well as writing material for the show.

NORMAN FLETCHER

PRISONER'S RECORD CARD

Name: **Norman Stanley Fletcher (known as Fletch)**	Prisoner No: **2215**
Home Address: 107 Alexandra Park Crescent, London N5	
Age: 42	

Family:
Married to Isobel (who used to work in the hardware department of a shop) while doing porridge. They stayed together twenty-four years. Has three children: Raymond, fourteen, Marion, nineteen, and twenty-four-year-old Ingrid, who was named after his mother, who in turn had been given the name of her mother's favourite film star, Ingrid Bergman. It's claimed that Fletcher's eldest daughter was conceived in Highgate Cemetery.

Length of Sentence:
Five years (transferred from Brixton), for robbery. After Post Office- and housebreaking, he decided to try his luck at something different: robbing a lorry. However, the brakes failed because it was over-loaded, and he crashed through three gardens and a brick wall before ending up in someone's tool shed.

Previous Form:
His entire life has been spent c/o Her Majesty's establishments, or so it seems. As a youngster he had a spell in Borstal, where he gained a diploma in plastering. Unfortunately, this earlier taste of prison life did little to prevent him turning into a jailbird: he served time at both Maidstone and Brixton prisons prior to Slade. Even his days as a schoolboy were spent at a special school because he was constantly playing truant.

His record is not surprising when you consider crime is in the blood of the Fletcher family. His great-granddad, William Wellington Fletcher, was the last person to be hung in England for sheep stealing.

PRISONER'S RECORD CARD

Background:
Earlier in his life, he adopted the name Frankie Fletcher and used to sing in clubs around North London. During the 1950s he was King of the Teds in Muswell Hill, where he grew up. In terms of siblings, we hear only of a brother, George, who sends him a Christmas card – illustrated with a naked lady because he's 'only allowed it once a year'!

Fletcher left school without any qualifications and, as he couldn't follow the careers he wanted (namely as a stockbroker, or a tennis coach at a girls' school), he declined the chance to work in a cardboard-box factory and instead robbed a sub Post Office off London's North Circular.

He did his national service in Malaya, working in the stores in Kuala Lumpur. His parents are still alive and recently celebrated their diamond wedding anniversary.

Personality:
Very droll, possessing a dry, sarcastic sense of humour – you need to watch him! Is also one of life's cynics.

Hobbies and Interests:
Passionate about film star Rita Hayworth. Studied carpentry while at Slade but was not the most successful of students.

Unusual Habits:
Frequently sings a line from the hit song 'You Belong to Me'. Gets a little irritating after a while, as does the constant gum-chewing.

Review of Time in Slade:
Treated with deference by fellow inmates, many of whom often turned to him for advice or when they needed a shoulder to cry on. Held several jobs at Slade: initially he was swilling out the pigs at the prison farm, then he worked in the library until an incident involving throwing a vicar off the balcony saw him transferred to a less cushy number. Got back into the governor's good books, though, and was assigned a job in the admin block.

Post-Prison Update:
After serving three and a half years of his sentence, Fletch was released from Slade only to find that his wife had left him. Lives in Muswell Hill with his daughter Ingrid and son Raymond. He has taken a job as a night porter, working from eleven to seven.

HM PRISON SLADE

Ronnie Barker

Ronnie Barker encountered no problems playing Fletcher, partly because he based some of the character's traits on himself. 'There was a lot of me in there – not that I break into post offices, of course!' Ronnie is eager to point out. 'There was plenty of my father in Fletch, too. Although the character was a Cockney and I was born in Oxford, he was working class and I could relate to him. He was easy to play and I didn't have to think much about it – unlike with Arkwright in *Open All Hours*, where I had to consider a different background entirely.

'Fletcher was obviously a wide-boy, out for everything he could get. Whatever he did was to his own benefit: you think he's helping someone out but he's working it to his own advantage; there are lots of examples of this in the scripts.' But Ronnie agrees that Fletch was likeable. 'You must always

have charm in a character. Even if you're playing an old tramp you need a bit of charm.'

Everyone involved in *Porridge* worked well together and found they could breeze through rehearsals. 'We'd often start at ten and finish by one because we all knew what we were doing,' says Ronnie, who knew he was carrying a lot of responsibility on his shoulders but never felt anything other than total support from those around him. 'You knew no one was going to let you down, ruin a gag or bit of timing.'

Upon reflection, Ronnie can spot certain milestones that acted as turning points in his long and exciting career. 'There are about five instances where I happened to be in the right place at the right time,' he says. 'I can't remember an occasion when I've been unlucky.' The first of these markers was his acceptance by a small repertory company in Aylesbury at the beginning of his career. Following this was his breakthrough to Oxford Rep, then his West End debut courtesy of Peter Hall. The other key moments involved his television career: appearing in *The Frost Report* alongside Ronnie Corbett was an important juncture, as Ronnie explains. 'As a result, David Frost signed us up for his production company; we had a five-year contract covering a sitcom and a series of *The Two Ronnies* each year. The show brought us into the limelight and helped establish our names with the Beeb.'

Ronnie was born in Bedford in 1929 and moved to Oxford at the age of four, when his father was relocated by Shell, for whom he was a clerk. Money was tight in the Barker household, but that didn't prevent Ronnie's father splashing out occasionally on a trip to the local theatre. His English master further encouraged his interest in the world of acting. 'It was during the Second World War, so the school was short-staffed because most of the teachers had joined the forces. A decision was taken not to continue with any theatre productions, but that didn't stop our English master doing a bit of reading in class. I remember playing the part of Shylock in *The Merchant of Venice* – it was great fun.'

Although he enjoyed the experience immensely, it wasn't until he'd left school and worked as clerk for a local bank that he acquired his taste for the stage. 'A pal I'd been at school with suggested I join a theatre group for something to do socially. He said: "There are a lot of girls there – and you don't need to be an actor; you can always help with the scenery."' But it wasn't long before Ronnie made his stage debut with The Theatre Players, his local amateur company. 'I was cast in a small part, then did a few more roles and suddenly realised it was what I wanted to do.'

After watching the Manchester Repertory Company perform at Aylesbury, Ronnie plucked up the courage to change direction and resign from the bank. 'I found the work very boring anyhow.' Ronnie's status as a junior clerk meant him being lumbered with many of the menial tasks. 'Everything had to be recorded by hand in thick ledgers, which terrified me – if you blotted them you were in terrible trouble.' He wrote a letter to the Aylesbury Rep asking for a job; and was soon employed as assistant stage manager, mainly working behind-the-scenes. Then: 'Within a couple of weeks I was offered a comedy part – and I can remember getting my first laugh even now.'

Ronnie found working in repertory theatre exhausting but exciting. 'While you were performing in one play, you'd also be rehearsing the next; and being involved in props meant I had to think about the one after that, too! But it was great training. Reps were wonderful because people came to see what actors and actresses were doing that week. They were more interested in the performers than the play, saying things like, "Oh, what's he playing?" or "Oh, look, he's got a moustache on this week."'

Ronnie feels that audiences in those pre-television days were much more naïve in their attitudes towards the trade than they are now. 'Audiences were less sophisticated. In the 1930s they'd say, "Let's go to that show in the West End where that man wears those funny suits." That was the height of the sophistication: they'd go and see a man in funny suits! The audiences were still a bit like that when I started, in 1948.'

PORRIDGE

It was evident from the start that Ronnie Barker had a natural talent for comedy; he enjoyed the genre and was skilled at it, even as a callow actor moving to Rhyl with the Aylesbury Rep.

When the company disbanded, Ronnie joined a rep at Bramhall, Cheshire, and there met Glenn Melvyn – who would later offer him his first taste of television, on *I'm Not Bothered*. But Ronnie at that time hankered after a return to his hometown, so wrote to the Oxford Playhouse and accepted a job in publicity as a way back. He went on to spend three years on the Playhouse stage before making his London and – shortly after – West End debuts.

The latter part of the 1950s saw Ronnie break into radio, with a regular role on *The Floggits* and parts on *Variety Playhouse* and *The Navy Lark*. He also made his film debut, as a head waiter in 1958's *Wonderful Things!* By the sixties, he was an established performer in all media, and the small screen had begun to take a higher priority in his career. While he made cameo appearances in dramas like *The Saint* and *The Avengers*, it was in *The Frost Report*, which began in 1966, and the equally irreverent *Not Only . . . But Also* that he established himself for television audiences. By now Ronnie had met the man who'd help him form one of television's strongest partnerships, *The Two Ronnies*, a relationship that would last twenty-two years.

In 1968, Ronnie was given his first series of pilot shows in *The Ronnie Barker Playhouse*. Three years later, *Six Dates with Barker* gave him the chance to experiment with a further batch. Although none of the pilot shows were picked up at that point, one was revisited nearly two decades later when Ronnie adapted Hugh Leonard's *The Removals Person* and created *Clarence*, the story of a short-sighted half-wit.

The sitcom turned out to be Ronnie's last, by which time he'd become one of comedy's true greats thanks to a body of work spanning the entire profession. 'I always thought the pilot would make a good series, so I rewrote the first episode to fit in with the rest that followed. I enjoyed making *Clarence*, partly because it was filmed around Oxfordshire.

The cottage featured in the series was built specially; it was beautiful and several people wanted to buy it.'

As well as for a dozen series of *The Two Ronnies* and numerous Christmas Specials, Ronnie is probably best remembered for playing Arkwright, the stingy shopkeeper in four series of *Open All Hours*, and Fletcher in *Porridge*. Unlike some actors, Ronnie Barker did not become typecast after appearing in a successful sitcom and has moved between roles with ease. He has, however, always worried about outstaying his welcome, and it was for this reason that he gave up his prison life as Fletch. 'I think Dick and Ian would have happily continued, but I didn't want to – although I agreed to do one more series [*Going Straight*] when Fletcher came out of prison.'

Ronnie feels he owes much to *Porridge*. 'It was probably the best and most important show I did, but *Open All Hours* topped it as far as fun was concerned. I loved doing both sitcoms but because of David Jason in *Open All Hours* it was slightly better, because of the laughs we had.

'I always worried about getting stuck with a character; I didn't want that. So after deciding to call it a day with *Porridge* I told Bill Cotton, Head of Comedy at that point, that I wanted to move on and do *Open All Hours*. He tried persuading me to stick with *Porridge* but it was no use.'

The first series of *Open All Hours* was recorded and transmitted in 1976 on BBC2, but it was five years before another series was seen. 'The first series only attracted about two and a half million viewers, which it would do on BBC2. I complained it was on the wrong channel, and when we finally made the second series it was shown on BBC1. It went on to become a massive hit.'

Ronnie has been the recipient of many awards in recognition of his services to the industry, including several BAFTAs. But none is more memorable than the award he collected at the Water Rats' Annual Dinner. 'It was an award for *Porridge*, so I thought it would be fun if I went in my uniform, handcuffed to Fulton. I asked him and he was delighted to do it. A limo was sent for us and just as we got to the venue we decided to put the handcuffs on – only to find we'd locked ourselves around a strap inside the car and couldn't get out. Eventually the chauffeur sorted that out.

'So in we went, and as we marched into the room there were great cheers and rounds of applause. But, although Fulton had the key, he couldn't open the cuffs. One of the people attending the dinner came up and said: 'Don't worry, I'm a member of the Magic Circle, I can get you out.' He spent twenty minutes trying but couldn't. We started to panic a bit but thankfully someone eventually prised us out of them.'

Ronnie Barker has now officially retired from the acting business. A number of factors were behind his decision. 'I'd run out of ideas and, to be honest, I'd done everything I wanted to do. And, I'm sorry to say, the material coming through wasn't such good quality.' As far as today's offerings on television are concerned, Ronnie isn't particularly impressed. 'I find it difficult to laugh at shows nowadays. I like programmes such as *As Time Goes By* and *Kiss Me Kate*, but I find some just too vulgar. Bad language in scripts can turn people away and much of it is unnecessary. 'One of the problems is that everyone wants to write their own scripts now; the performers write and feel they have to resort to lines concerning bodily functions. Producers are trying desperately to appeal to younger viewers, but they're not watching television – they're out with their chums. Producers should concentrate on older viewers if they want to increase audience figures.'

LENNIE GODBER

PRISONER'S RECORD CARD

Name: **Leonard Arthur Godber (known as Lennie)**	Prisoner No: **3470**

Home Address:
Not disclosed

Age:
23

Family:
Single, although had a fiancée, Denise, when incarcerated. This relationship fizzled out during his time behind bars. Lennie's mother was relieved at the split as she never liked Denise, partly because she wore green nail-varnish and went around braless!

Length of Sentence:
Two years, for breaking and entering.

Previous Form:
First offender, although he was lucky not to have been caught for a previous offence. He was planning to turn over a house in Sutton Coldfield where the chimney was his only source of access. He ended up getting stuck and his intended victims arrived home to find his legs sticking out of the fireplace. He managed to escape, but as a result of the incident he now suffers from claustrophobia.

HM PRISON SLADE

PRISONER'S RECORD CARD

Background:

Grew up in a Birmingham back street, but Godber is proud of his upbringing because his mother kept her children spotless despite money being scarce. He is very close to his mother, but doesn't know where his father is.

Personality:

A likeable, hard-working prisoner, although easily led. A little naïve.

Hobbies and Interests:

Interested in making up for lost time and improving on the one O level (geography) he holds. Attended as many classes as possible while at Slade, including pottery and elementary plumbing. Also studied for a history O level.

A keen footballer and follower of Aston Villa, his favourite television programme is Kojak.

Unusual Habits:

Doesn't drink tea and dislikes brown toast!

Review of Time in Slade:

A quiet, conscientious prisoner who worked in the kitchen during his sentence.

Post-Prison Update:

Since his release, Godber has moved back to Birmingham. He secured employment as a long-distance lorry driver but spent more and more time in Muswell Hill, courting none other than Fletcher's daughter Ingrid. He would annoy Fletcher by parking an articulated lorry outside his home, blocking the sunlight from entering the windows. Ended up marrying Ingrid and honeymooning in Lanzarote.

Richard Beckinsale

Richard Beckinsale's sudden death at the age of thirty-one was tragic. Not only did it rob his family of a loving husband and father, but it also deprived the world of showbusiness of one of its greatest talents, an actor whose career promised even greater things than he'd already achieved. Actor Christopher Biggins worked alongside Richard in several episodes of Porridge and admired his talent. 'He would have moved through each decade and have become, in my view, a huge name – he'd probably have become a movie star by now.'

With several hit shows under his belt, Richard was a sought-after actor, particularly in the world of television. Although he held a desire to expand his portfolio of characterisations beyond the naïve, callow, likeable men he was usually asked to play, his portrayal of such roles was always top class, his abilities affording him seamless performances.

When he was interviewed back in the seventies by Yorkshire Television, Richard expressed his desire to progress to more mature roles. With *The Lovers* and *Rising Damp* each showing him as an impressionable young man, he said, 'I'm getting a bit old for this type of role. I want to play older parts.' But he always made a success of the comedy roles he played, and never regretted accepting roles like Alan in *Rising Damp*, Geoffrey in *The Lovers* and, of course, Lennie Godber in *Porridge*. 'I've always been selective, especially where comedy series are concerned. I have been lucky in that I accepted three offers in television comedy within a relatively short space of time that became hits. But I have also turned down several offers which I feel pretty sure would not have been hits.'

Tony Osoba, who became friends with Richard during the days of *Porridge*, was aware he was keen to progress to more mature roles, but points out that the reason he was continuously offered such jobs was because he played them so well. 'We didn't know each other that well beforehand, even though we both played football for a showbusiness team and had a few mutual friends; but, as the show went along, we got to know each other better and began socialising quite a bit.

'Part of that shy naïveté came from Richard, but there was a lot more to his acting than that. And one of the great things about him was that you could watch him and never see him act, which is an art. It appeared that he was doing it effortlessly and whatever character he played was real; that's a superb skill because it isn't easy.

'In Godber, he had a character who was much more than just a foil for Fletcher. He had to explore a range of emotions: there were moments where he had to be strong, others where he was struggling coming to terms with prison and had to be helped along; Richard conveyed that superbly.'

Born in Nottingham in 1947, Richard left school at sixteen determined to become an actor. Before his dream came true, he worked as an upholsterer, in an iron-pipe factory and as a clerk in the accounts department at the local gas board, while studying English and art at night school. But when he was offered a place at RADA in 1966, he headed for London and a new career.

After graduating from drama school, Richard – whose daughters Kate and Samantha are both actresses – worked in rep, initially at Crewe, before more extensive theatre roles came his way, such as that of Romeo in a production of *Romeo and Juliet* at the Leeds Playhouse in 1971. He was soon offered a number of small parts on television, including one in a 1969 episode of *Coronation Street* (playing PC Wilcox, he was responsible for arresting Ena Sharples).

But his big break came in 1970, when alongside Paula Wilcox he played Geoffrey in Granada's sitcom *The Lovers*. Two series were transmitted and his performance as the young Mancunian bank clerk won him an award as Best TV Newcomer for 1971. The show became a big hit with viewers and, by the time *Porridge* and *Rising Damp* – in which he played medical student Alan – were up and running in the mid-1970s, Richard Beckinsale had become a household name. Other television credits included *Couples, Second House, Tales of Piccadilly, Elephant Eggs in a Rhubarb Tree, Give and Take, Truscott's Luck* and *Consequences*.

Although the success he achieved in sitcom brought security, Richard was always on the hunt for fresh challenges on screen and stage. In 1975 he was offered a straight role in the TV film *Last Summer*, while the theatre saw him in productions of Shakespeare as well as in various musicals and satires. In 1979 he'd moved on to a new BBC sitcom, *Bloomers*, written by James Saunders, when he suffered a fatal heart attack. Rehearsals were due to begin on the sixth episode of the series when he died suddenly at his home; the five episodes already recorded were later transmitted with the blessing of his widow, actress Judy Loe.

Christopher Biggins recalls the moment he heard about Richard's death. 'I was making a film called *The Tempest* for Derek Jarman. We were filming in Northumberland and were staying in this rickety old hotel. It was freezing cold and I was having a lie down after filming on the beaches, when suddenly the manager came to me and said: "Mr Biggins, the *Sun* newspaper wants a comment from you." When I asked him on what subject, he replied: "Richard Beckinsale has just died." I was totally gobsmacked and could not believe it.'

News of Beckinsale's death was equally shocking for Ronnie Barker to accept. It was producer Sydney Lotterby who told him about the tragic event. 'He phoned and simply said, "Richard's dead!" I didn't understand what he was saying at first so he repeated himself. I couldn't believe what I was hearing. As far as I know he hadn't had anything wrong with his heart. We'd just finished the film and we'd both undergone insurance medicals, which we'd passed. It was such a shock.'

MR MACKAY

PRISON OFFICER'S EMPLOYMENT CARD

Name: **Mr Mackay**	Job Title: **Senior Prison Officer**
Age: 55	
Length of Service: Twenty-five years	

Family:
Married for seventeen years. Seems a happy marriage, especially as his wife regularly presses his uniform!

Background:
Endured a tough childhood in the shadows of the Lanarkshire coal-fields. Money was scarce, so through necessity he left school at fourteen and became a boy soldier in order to help pay the bills in his impoverished household – although one of the prisoners, Fletcher, always claimed it was really a way of hiding behind a 'mantle of security'. His father was almost permanently unemployed, a depressing situation with eight children to support.

During the sixteen years he served with the 1st Battalion of the Argyll and Sutherland Highlanders, he climbed the promotion ladder to the rank of sergeant major. He also served as a drill sergeant, and travelled to far-flung corners of the world, including Malaya.

When he eventually returned to life as a civilian, he ran a boarding house, The Strathclyde, with his wife for two years (1951–53) in Peebles. The venture was far from successful, swallowing up most of Mackay's savings and demob pay, so he sold up. After a failed attempt to re-enlist, he plumped for the prison service instead.

HM PRISON
SLADE

PRISON OFFICER'S EMPLOYMENT CARD

Personality:
Parades around like a peacock, with a back so rigid it wouldn't be a surprise to find a board stuffed up his jacket!

Hobbies and Interests:
Few: it appears that the prison service is his life. However, he has a history in boxing, having fought for Midlothian Boys and for his army battalion.

Unusual Habits:
Has an infuriating habit of wrenching his neck at moments of confrontation or stress.

Suitability for Job:
Ran Slade Prison with a fist of iron, but it wouldn't do any harm if he were to adopt a more contemporary attitude towards how the establishment should be run. A little sense of humour wouldn't go amiss either.

Stop Press! In contrast to the meteoric climb up the promotion ladder he probably expected, Mackay left the service after a quarter of a century without reaching the ranks of management and with a bitter taste in his mouth.

HM PRISON
SLADE

Fulton Mackay

Such is the power of television, Fulton Mackay will always be remembered for playing his televisual namesake in Porridge. His top-notch portrayal of Slade Prison's stern warder may have been an early excursion into small-screen comedy, but the versatile Scottish actor had for years previously plied his trade in the theatre. When he pulled on his warder's uniform for the first time it was clear his had been a piece of first-class casting. Ronnie Barker enjoyed playing alongside Fulton. 'He was immensely likeable, a charming man, while in character he was the person you loved to hate. Fulton had plenty of charisma and I thought he played the part impeccably.' But Ronnie always wondered where Fulton thought his character was supposed to be from. 'He told me he based the character on a PT instructor he'd encountered in the forces, a man who used to swagger about, but Fulton always did a strange accent that wasn't quite Scottish – I never dared ask him whether it was Cockney.'

A smile crosses Ronnie's face as he recalls how Fulton bagged most of the rehearsal time. 'He was a great actor but occasionally would say, "I can't play this scene, Ronnie." About three-quarters of the rehearsal time was devoted to him, which initially I didn't mind. But eventually I had to say things like: "In this episode I've got twenty-five minutes, you've got five, so can I do a bit of rehearsing as well?"'

Someone else who experienced Fulton's attention to detail was Sam Kelly, who played Warren, one of the inmates at Slade Prison. 'He put in a brilliant performance as Mr Mackay. He'd come from years of serious, straight Scottish theatre, yet took to comedy like a duck to water. But he was very pernickety – I remember one day sitting in the producer's box with Syd Lotterby, who shouted: "Oh, come on, Fulton, for God's sake!" Fulton couldn't hear him, of course, but he was absolutely furious with him over something – and I suspect that sort of thing went on more often than we knew. Although Fulton was very particular, the end result was extremely good.'

Jimmy Gilbert, Head of Comedy at the Beeb when *Porridge* was commissioned, became a close friend of Fulton's and believes any domination in terms of rehearsal time was due to his quest for perfection. 'He was a total perfectionist and very self-critical,' says Jimmy. 'Perfectionists can sometimes be a bit prickly – and Fulton *could* be difficult, but he was a delightful man. As a friend he was such fun and very loyal; I regarded him as family.'

Fulton was born in Paisley, Renfrewshire, in 1922. His mother died when he was just a boy so, with his father working in the NAAFI, an aunt in Clydebank raised him. Upon leaving school, he was employed as a quantity surveyor for a time before volunteering for the RAF in 1941. But a perforated eardrum prevented him from joining up and he turned instead to the army, going on to complete five years' service, three of which were spent in India.

On his return to civvy street, he enrolled at RADA in 1945; after graduating he embarked on a theatrical career, working many years in rep, including nine seasons at Glasgow's Citizens' Theatre. He was also employed at Edinburgh's Royal Lyceum Theatre before offers of work in London came his way, beginning at the Arts Theatre Club, where in 1960 he appeared in *Naked Island*, a production about POWs in Singapore. Between 1962 and 1963 he worked for the Old Vic Company, while a spell with the Royal Shakespeare Company involved playing Squeers in the original production of the Company's *The Life and Adventures of Nicholas Nickleby*.

His talents extended to writing, and he contributed plays for BBC radio and television, including *Girl with Flowers in Her Hair* and *Semper Fidelis*. He also appeared in several films, including *Local Hero*, with Burt Lancaster, *The Brave Don't Cry, Gumshoe, Defence of the Realm, Nothing But the Night, Laxdale Hall* and *Britannia Hospital*. He made many small-screen appearances, too: among his credits are roles in *Some Mothers Do 'Ave 'Em, Three Fables of Orkney*, a series of *Special Branch, Ghosts, The*

Troubleshooters, Master of Ballantrae, Clay, Slip-Up, A Sense of Freedom, The Foundation, The Palace and Going Gently. But, despite his prolific career, Fulton Mackay will always be remembered by most for his portrayal of Slade Prison's strict disciplinarian.

Away from acting, one of Fulton's passions was art, as Tony Osoba, who struck up a friendship with Fulton during the filming of *Porridge*, explains. 'I think it might surprise some people to know that Fulton – who many people think of as this tough, rugged prison officer – enjoyed sitting in his garden painting pictures of flowers and trees. He was a very private man, so I felt privileged when he invited me to his home where he showed me his collection of paintings. Fulton was also a writer, and completed several romantic plays about Scotland.'

Fulton died in 1987, aged sixty-four. It was a shock to everyone, not least to close friend Jimmy Gilbert. 'I was heading off to the Montreux Film Festival and saw Fulton just before leaving. He said he was going into hospital to have an operation but made light of it. I remember saying to him, "For God sake, don't do something silly like keeling over." He laughed and said he'd see me when I returned. By the time I got back he'd had the operation, but it turned out to be stomach cancer and he died within a week. I miss him dearly.'

Fulton has left a legacy of fine portrayals on stage and screen; but, in terms of television comedy, it's difficult to find a better piece of work than his rich, colourful creation known as Mr Mackay.

MR BARROWCLOUGH

PRISON OFFICER'S EMPLOYMENT CARD

Name: **Henry Barrowclough**	Job Title: **Prison Officer**
Age: Not prepared to divulge such personal information.	
Length of Service: Twenty-three years' unblemished service.	

Family:

Unhappily married to Alice. Has openly admitted that the 'sun rarely shines in his household', which partly explains his brief affair with Dorothy Jamieson, the Governor's secretary.

His wife doesn't like his job; nor where they live, missing the amenities offered by a city. Barrowclough has painted a rather grue-some picture of her, claiming she's bitter, restless, bad-tempered and has spots. Their marriage has been on the rocks for some time, and she's enjoyed liaisons with other men – most recently with a marriage counsellor. To Barrowclough's dismay, invariably, she soon returns.

Background:

Refers to his background as 'a bit of a mixture', probably because previous generations of the Barrowclough family contain Scottish, English, Irish and Polish blood running through their veins. His granddad was an ironmonger in Accrington.

Completed national service with the RAF in Singapore, working in the equipment section, before joining the prison service – something he claimed he did because of always wanting a vocation that would 'satisfy his desire to do work of public usefulness'. (However, it's also been rumoured that the free house and uniform were key motivations behind his application.)

HM PRISON SLADE

PRISON OFFICER'S EMPLOYMENT CARD

Personality:

Described by prisoner 2215 (Fletcher) as looking like 'Arthur Askey on stilts'.

Hobbies and Interests:

Has a passion for astronomy and botany. Occasionally takes prisoners out on to the fell to explore the countryside.

Unusual Habits:

None known.

Suitability for Job:

Never going to set the prison-service career ladder on fire! Views himself as a modern-day humanitarian but his beliefs are occasionally far from considered. A bit wet, he's far too easily led and influenced to be considered for demanding managerial responsibilities.

He's an overly nervous individual who believes he's got an inferiority complex. He also feels he's holding down his job by the skin of his teeth, and has visited the prison psychiatric unit because of his lack of self-confidence.

HM PRISON SLADE

Brian Wilde

Brian Wilde believes Mackay and Barrowclough probably reflected the culture within the prison service at the time of Porridge's first run. 'You had the old hard-bitten warders who felt prisoners were inside to be punished, and a new wave of officers coming through who were interested in rehabilitating prisoners.'

Brian knew early on that *Porridge* possessed the necessary ingredients for success. 'The writers were excellent; they knew what they were doing and made it easier for the actors to play their characters. The series was also well cast, even down to the smaller parts; then we had Syd Lotterby, a very good director and excellent at casting, who was helped by an excellent assistant, Judy Loe. When you put it all together it's not surprising the show worked so well.'

When asked to select a favourite episode, Brian quickly points to 'Prisoner and Escort', the pilot which afforded him the lion's share of the scenes with Ronnie Barker. 'I had lots to do in it, whereas in other episodes I wasn't given so much,' he says, admittedly disappointed that his character wasn't allowed to develop to the extent he would have wished. 'In the series, Barrowclough wasn't as important as in the pilot, which was sad.'

Away from his duties patrolling the landings at Slade Prison, Mr Barrowclough endured a miserable home life. So unhappy was the warder, he'd even open his heart to Fletcher about his tribulations, conjuring up the worst possible images of his insufferable wife – who we never saw. 'It was left to the audience to use their imagination about what she looked like. To have shown her would have ruined the effect.'

Reflecting on his time playing Slade's ineffectual warder, Brian feels that overall it was a happy period in his career. 'We had a good company. You can't spend a lot of time with people without either falling out bitterly or getting on; fortunately we all got on well together.'

When *Porridge* came to an end in 1977, it was a sad time for the cast who'd worked together during three series and two Christmas Specials. But Brian acknowledges that the time was right to call it a day. 'There's nothing worse than letting a series drag on and I think it stopped at just the right time, when the episodes were still strong.' He wasn't so keen on the film, though. 'I don't think it worked and it had an air of tiredness about it.'

Two long-running, highly successful characters have dominated Brian's career: Barrowclough in *Porridge* and Foggy in *Last of the Summer Wine*. Brian again refers to the quality of the scripts as the reason behind the latter show's phenomenal success. 'Actors depend so much on the people who write the scripts and Roy Clarke was another good author. It makes life so much easier if the script tells you what to do, is clear and watertight. You then have confidence in the programme.'

He first appeared as Foggy in 1976 and stayed eight years before taking a break from the show. In 1990 he returned to the fold but eventually a minor indisposition forced him to give up the role.

As well as long-running parts in two of Britain's most popular sitcoms, Brian's TV career has included a debut in 1951's *Black Limelight*, Sir Thomas Landers in 1954's *The Scarlet Pimpernel*, a cemetery attendant in 1961's *Jango*, Happy Dwyer in a 1964 episode of *The Protectors*, several roles in *The Man in Room 17* a year later and appearances in *The Avengers, The Dustbinmen, Out of the Unknown, The Sweeney, The Love of Mike, Elizabeth R* and the lead in *Wyatt's Watchdogs*. Unfortunately the 1988 sitcom about a retired army major who formed a neighbourhood watch only lasted one series. 'We tried it but it didn't work for some reason – it was a good idea, though.'

Lancashire-born Brian grew up in Hertfordshire before training at RADA. But his life as a professional actor couldn't have got off to a worse start when he spent six months unemployed. He finally earned his first wage packet on stage at St Andrew's in Scotland before joining Liverpool Rep. The swift turnaround of plays in repertory theatre afforded Brian the chance to play different characters – a rich learning curve for any actor, though he wasn't conscious of it at the time. 'You just play the roles and hope it helps, but most of the time you didn't have time to think about how valuable it might all be.'

During the fifties and sixties he worked extensively in the theatre, with credits including *The Power and the Glory, The Ring of Truth, The Visit* and Peter Ustinov's *The Moment of Truth*, which was the first West End production in which Brian had a 'decent' part. He was the first member of his family to tread the boards. 'If anyone else in the family had done it I probably wouldn't have, because I'd have spotted all the pitfalls. I knew nothing about them, so I went in with every confidence – then realised what a hit-and-miss profession it is: you may click or may not. I thank God for the marvellous opportunities I had in *Porridge* and *Last of the Summer Wine*.'

After years of gaining what were mainly cameo roles in TV – in shows like *Doomwatch* and *Our Mutual Friend* – the two sitcoms meant Brian was thrust suddenly into the media spotlight and his career duly rewarded. 'I was doing quite well but it was nice to have something more than the odd episode here and there. It's lovely having regular work, because you feel more secure and can get on with acting instead of worrying.'

As well as working on the stage and television, Brian has appeared in a handful of films, such as *Simon and Laura, Street Corner, Will Any Gentleman . . .?, Tiger in the Smoke, Night of the Demon, Girls at Sea, On the Run, Rattle of a Simple Man, Darling, The Informers, Carry On Doctor, One Brief Summer* and *The Jokers*. While the latter part of his career has been dominated by comedy – particularly on TV – his early appearances were mainly in dramas. 'I used to play a lot of heavies at one time,' he admits.

He's quick to brush off the significance of his film roles, regarding them as 'inconsequential', and didn't particularly enjoy working in the medium. 'My appearances were just spits and coughs, nothing to speak of. Although I had a reasonable part in *The Jokers*, the rest were just one- or two-day jobs, so insignificant I can't remember them.'

Looking back over his long career, he finds it difficult choosing a favourite medium. 'I enjoy television but there's nothing like the excitement of the theatre, especially when the curtain goes up: you see the audience waiting for you, and you know you've got to get on with it and make it work.' Conversely, however, Brian's desires these days have changed: 'I don't work in the theatre because I couldn't stand the boredom of performing the same play every night, whereas in television you record a scene and it's over.' Today, Brian is semi-retired and taking life a little easier. 'I'm not actively seeking work – but if something interesting on TV came along, I'd consider it.'

THE WRITERS ON THE ACTORS

Clement on Barker

When I was set to direct my first movie, *Otley*, I tried to cast Ronnie as a professional assassin – the part eventually played by Leonard Rossiter. I was looking for a superb comic actor, my theory being that if you can play comedy you can play anything.

I still believe that. I wish we had seen Ronnie extend himself more as an actor because I never saw limits to his talent. He brought with him a rare intelligence. First to the script, where his quick mind offered up new or improved jokes, always with great respect. 'Is that all right?' he'd ask and as a rule, once we'd stopped laughing, we'd nod okay. When blocking a scene he was ahead of me as a director, usually sensing where the camera had to be for the master shot.

The day of the taping made him nervous. He didn't like to 'warm up' the studio audience, needing to concentrate on the job in hand. Yet once under way, if something went wrong, he was the one who stepped into the breach, explaining the problem and making them laugh.

Many actors are thrown off balance by the audience. They rehearse all week without them and then their response on the day of the taping throws their timing completely. It's a strange, hybrid medium – an awkward cross between theatre and film. But I can think of nobody who worked a studio audience better than Ronnie.

Take a moment in the pilot episode, 'Prisoner and Escort', when Fletcher, having been on the moors all night, discovers at dawn that he is back where he started from. We artfully concealed this fact from the studio audience and it got a huge laugh. But watch the tape and see what wonders Ronnie did with the moment.

Other actors would have got two laughs out of it – he got three. And without mugging or going out of character.

Porridge was the perfect marriage of an actor to a part. It was not the series Ronnie had envisaged – he'd seen it more as a prison version of *Bilko*. But once we'd gone round Wandsworth, Brixton and the Scrubs we knew we couldn't write that. For a while we didn't know how to write anything. Perhaps what kept us going was the thought that at a certain point Ronnie Barker was going to appear and the audience, at home as well as in the studio, would relax, knowing they were in safe hands – the hands of a comic genius.

He's also a warm and generous friend. After the *Porridge* movie, when he went to Australia for a year, he gave Ian and me his Jaguar! I think I drove it on odd days and Ian on even ones. In those days Ronnie usually had at least three years work planned in advance. He'd struggled in the early years and seemed to fear unemployment. Then suddenly, just after Peter Hall asked him to play Falstaff at the National, he decided to stop completely. I've never really understood why and I think it's a great loss. But thank you, Ronnie, for the great pleasure you have given all of us. And the Jaguar – though it needed a new silencer. Did I ever mention that?

La Frenais on Beckinsale

Richard didn't seem like any actor I'd ever met. By *Porridge* I'd been 'around' actors for a few years and as much as I loved and respected them, found them a breed of complex contradictions: self-absorbed and neurotic, obnoxious, vulnerable, ambitious and humble, egotistical and insecure; not surprising given the nature of their profession in which rejection is an inevitable constant.

Richard was different, and whatever drove him didn't appear to be fuelled by ambition and ego. He was the typical 'great bloke' that you remembered fondly from school. The one who stayed in the same home town, the same steady job and in the same marriage and whose view of the world was completely free of envy or malice.

The term 'laid back' didn't exist in the mid-seventies, but if it had there would have been a picture of Richard next to the dictionary definition. He was a terrible reader, which is the first part of an actor's investiture in a new role: the moment when he has nothing but a notion of the character and the unread, 'cold' script. Richard was hopeless, it's a wonder that he progressed from his earliest auditions!

He was even bad after he'd had the script for a few days and we all assembled for the cast read-through. Then something amazing happened, as it did every week when Richard's performances went from hesitancy and incoherence to the truth and brilliance with which he invested all his work. His acting, like himself, was without artifice or guile. He left the stage ridiculously early and I think his talent was irreplaceable.

Clement on Mackay

Fulton was a lovely man, brim full of life, love and enthusiasm. A well-rounded, spiritual man. Syd Lotterby told me that Fulton would rehearse forever if you let him, never too tired to have another try to see if he could make his performance even better. It was true, but it came from a deep desire for perfection, and at the same time a zestful energy for doing something he loved.

He did certain things in *Porridge* which were inimitable. I think of Mr Mackay's reaction when he knows Fletcher has put one over on him – first a cold fury that he's been had, followed by a mute warning of dire retribution to come. Ian and I can always make each other laugh by remembering his reading of a line from the movie, where he's showing the ropes to a new screw. 'The prison officers have a club. It is *known* . . . [a long, drawn out emphasis on this word, while his left hand paints the title on an imaginary door] . . . as The Prison Officers' Club.'

When an actor makes a part his own to that degree you can't imagine how you ever wrote it in the first place without seeing him in your mind's eye. I think it took us a few shows before we realised what a priceless asset he was, and what a brilliant adversary for Fletcher.

But I remember him, too, as a painter and philosopher, enormously kind and ever optimistic. I really miss him.

La Frenais on Wilde

The casting of *Porridge* was astonishing. Remember it wasn't the pilot episode of an intended series with all the pressure that entails, when the stakes are so much higher and every decision comes under so much scrutiny. 'Prisoner and Escort' was devised as a 'one off' play, in a series of seven whose only common link was that each would showcase Ronnie Barker's remarkable talent. If we'd known it was a series would the casting process have been more intense or selective? I can't imagine it could have been more perfect, and it was a brilliant achievement for producer Syd Lotterby.

Brian belonged to that stock of character actors whose work, understated and subtle, is consistently excellent and consistently unheralded. I think of Brian as the civil servant overlooked for his expected promotion; the man in the raincoat at the bus stop who's jostled aside and left standing in the rain. Or the clerk who lives with his invalid mother and who pines secretly, and hopelessly, for the girl in the accounts department.

Brian's characters don't stand out in the crowd. They blend in with the background, camouflaged against the spotlight. A little like the man himself whom we never got to know really well but grew to respect with growing affection for his dry humour and superb acting instincts.

Inevitably, the success of the series did thrust Brian more into the spotlight, as much as he tried to shield himself from its transitory glare. But at least a large and enthusiastic public got to recognise his craft and his talent.

He brought much more to the character of Barrowclough than I think, in truth, Dick and I put on the page. It was too easy just to be a patsy to Fletcher's cunning or the downtrodden husband. Brian ennobled Mister Barrowclough with compassion, and a sweet-natured perseverance that never allowed him to be pitiful or ridiculous. With his furrowed brow and lugubrious features he made us laugh unexpectedly, and frequently. And he did so by finding the truth of the character. And his humanity.

EPISODE GUIDE – *PORRIDGE*

Original transmission: **Thursday 5 September 1974, BBC1, 8.30 p.m.**

CAST

Norman Fletcher	**Ronnie Barker**
Mr Barrowclough	**Brian Wilde**
Mr Mackay	**Fulton Mackay**
Lennie Godber	**Richard Beckinsale**
Cyril Heslop	**Brian Glover**
Medical Officer	**John Bennett**
The Governor	**Michael Barrington**
Other Prison Officers	**Ronald Musgrove**
. . . .	**Edward Cogdale**
. . . .	**Keith Norrish**

Mackay introduces three new arrivals to life at Slade Prison: while Cyril Heslop and Norman Fletcher are old hands, Lennie Godber is a first offender, so Mackay asks Fletch to describe a typical day, beginning at 7 a.m. with a 'persistent and deafening bell'.

After their possessions are confiscated – a process Fletcher describes as their 'dehumanisation' – he helps Godber come to terms with his predicament and tries convincing him he can survive the 'grim nightmare of his next two years'.

No longer a novice to prison life, Fletch expects special attention, perhaps even his own cell, and one that's south-facing! But there's a shock in store when he discovers Godber is allocated his own cell and he's forced to share with Heslop and the electric light-bulb-eating Evans. Just to rub salt into the wound, Godber and Heslop are given cushy jobs while Fletch is assigned pig-swilling duties.

WHAT A SCENE!

**Three new arrivals (Fletcher, Godber and Heslop) are
standing to attention, while Mr Mackay looks out
through the barred windows.**

MACKAY

What a beautiful day, for the time of year, quite astonishing. Beautiful day.

FLETCHER

(Sarcastically) Oh, lovely. Perhaps we can go out later on
for a cycle ride!

Original transmission: **Thursday 12 September 1974**
BBC1, 8.30 p.m.

CAST

Norman Fletcher . . . . **Ronnie Barker**
Mr Barrowclough . . . . **Brian Wilde**
Mr Mackay . . . . **Fulton Mackay**
Lennie Godber . . . . **Richard Beckinsale**
Heslop . . . . **Brian Glover**
Ives . . . . **Ken Jones**
Lukewarm . . . . **Christopher Biggins**
Evans . . . . **Ray Dunbobbin**
Mr Appleton . . . . **Graham Ashley**
Prison Officer . . . . **John Quarmby**

Gambling is rife inside Slade Prison. Prisoners are so desperate for a flutter they'll bet on anything, including flies crawling up the wall and which hymns will be sung in the chapel. So it's good news when Fletch receives permission from Grouty to run a dice game.

On Saturday afternoon, while the warders challenge E Wing to a football match, a gathering of prisoners in the boiler room roll the dice. But Ives, who wasn't allowed to participate, has bet eight ounces of snout against them completing the game before the warders find out. Angry at being excluded from the game, he seeks revenge by informing Mackay of Fletch's illegal game of snakes and ladders; but instead of storming the secret location, the Chief Warder awaits a delivery of coal to help him out!

WHAT A SCENE!

Fletcher is organising some betting. He chats to Godber.

GODBER
What do you play for, big stakes?

FLETCHER
Yeah, if we can nick any out of the meat safe, yeah.

91

SERIES ONE   A NIGHT IN

Original transmission: 📺 **Thursday 19 September 1974**
BBC1, 8.30 p.m.

CAST

Norman Fletcher . . . . **Ronnie Barker**
Lennie Godber . . . . **Richard Beckinsale**
Prison Officer . . . . **Paul McDowell**

Fletch's peace is shattered when he's forced to share his cell
with Lennie Godber, but they settle down after pointing out
all the rules. It's not long before Godber is confiding in
Fletch, telling him how he's struggling to adapt to terms with
life inside – especially as he's got 698 days to go! He's also
worried whether his fiancée, Denise, will wait for him.

During the long, cold night the two inmates discuss the
woes of the world. Fletch reminds Godber about the importance of dreams, where there are 'no locked doors' to restrict
the imagination, and helps his young cellmate survive the
night, marking the beginning of a strong friendship.

WHAT A SCENE!

**Godber, who has to share Fletch's cell, discusses his
old cellmate, Banks, who caused a riot on his landing.**

GODBER

He smuggled this kitten into his cell and from the way
he handled it you could see the gentle side of his nature.

FLETCHER

You what? Before he lit his mattress I heard he threw a
screw off the top landing.

GODBER

Well he wasn't hurt, he hit the safety net.

Original transmission: 📺 **Thursday 26 September 1974**
BBC1, 8.30 p.m.

CAST

Norman Fletcher	**Ronnie Barker**
Mr Barrowclough	**Brian Wilde**
Mr Mackay	**Fulton Mackay**
Lennie Godber	**Richard Beckinsale**
Ives	**Ken Jones**
Navy Rum	**Paul Angelis**
Dylan	**Philip Jackson**
Scrounger	**Johnny Wade**
Vicar	**Robert Gillespie**
Verger	**John Rutland**
Chief Prison Officer	**Arnold Peters**
Landlord	**Ralph Watson**
Nurse	**Peggy Mason**

Fletcher and Godber enjoy the fresh air when they join a
party digging drainage ditches for the council. Under
Mackay's strict supervision the men keep on task, but when
he pops down to the local village to buy spare parts for his
lawnmower – a good excuse for a quick snifter –
Barrowclough is put in charge.

True to form, the men take advantage of the situation.
When Ives gets stung on the behind and writhes in agony,
Fletch persuades Barrowclough to let him dash down to the
village to fetch medication. Borrowing a quid from the
gullible warder, he heads for the nearest pub, but as he sinks
a drink Mackay appears on the scene and Fletch has to make
a quick exit. But there's more drama in store before the day
is out.

WHAT A SCENE!

Fletch and Godber discuss why they're pleased to be spending a day away from Slade Prison.

FLETCHER

Yeah, I must admit, I'm looking forward to going out today, yeah, yeah. Get the smell of disinfectant out of my nostrils – not to mention your festering feet!

GODBER

I change my socks every day.

FLETCHER

Oh yeah. Pity you can't change your feet, innit?

Original transmission: **Thursday 3 October 1974**
BBC1, 8.30 p.m.

CAST

Norman Fletcher . . . . **Ronnie Barker**
Mr Barrowclough . . . . **Brian Wilde**
Mr Mackay . . . . **Fulton Mackay**
Ives . . . . **Ken Jones**
The Governor . . . . **Michael Barrington**
McLaren . . . . **Tony Osoba**

After upsetting Mr Mackay, Fletch is stripped of his cushy
farm job and forced to make fishing nets. Needlework
wreaks havoc with his hands, so he asks Barrowclough –
who owes him a favour after accepting his advice on
domestic affairs – to secure him a job in the library.

Fletch tries hard getting back into the Governor's good
books, but also finds time to tender advice to McLaren
about curbing his aggressive nature, which sees him
red-carded for the third time in four football matches.
McLaren's anger overspills and he climbs on to the prison
roof and won't come down until his demands are met.
Spotting an opportunity to ingratiate himself with the
Governor, Fletch comes to the rescue – with a little help
from McLaren himself – and ends up being rewarded with
his job in the library.

WHAT A SCENE!

McLaren and Fletch have a confrontation. Fletch loses his temper and grabs him.

FLETCHER

I don't want no trouble with you, McLaren. Listen to me, you. I know you're a hard case, we all know that. We all know you're full of nasty militant feelings, but if you ever talk to me again like that I'm going to twist your head round like a cork in a bottle of Beaujolais, all right?

MCLAREN

Yes.

FLETCHER

I'm going to pull it off and give it to that poof in B Wing to keep his wigs on.

Original transmission: Thursday 10 October 1974
BBC1, 8.30 p.m.

CAST

Norman Fletcher	**Ronnie Barker**
Mr Barrowclough	**Brian Wilde**
Mr Mackay	**Fulton Mackay**
Warren	**Sam Kelly**
Heslop	**Brian Glover**
The Governor	**Michael Barrington**
Lukewarm	**Christopher Biggins**
Sergeant Norris	**Royston Tickner**
Tolly	**Emlyn Price**
Isobel	**June Ellis**
Ingrid Fletcher	**Patricia Brake**
Norma	**Susan Littler**
Iris	**Andonia Katsaros**
Elaine	**Rosalind Elliot**
Trevor	**Donald Groves**

When the illiterate Warren, a fellow inmate, receives a letter from his wife, he asks Fletcher to read it. It's clear from the downbeat tone that his beloved's affections have strayed. Fletch tells a group of lags that Warren's letter is indicative of a woman's state of mind when her hubby has been inside between eight and twelve months; he claims that, although they make their vows, it's difficult to prevent them straying.

With visiting day approaching, Fletcher drafts a letter and suggests his friends send it to their loved ones, feeling confident the subtlety of his writing will do the trick.

Warren believes Fletch's letter has done the trick when he receives a reassuring reply, suggesting he has nothing to worry about. All the wives turn up on visiting day – except Fletcher's. His daughter Ingrid arrives instead to break the news that his wife has run off with a heating engineer who drives a mustard-coloured Ford Capri!

Fletcher is so stunned that the prison's welfare officer recommends forty-eight hours' compassionate leave to help sort matters out. Escorted home by Sergeant Norris of the local constabulary, Fletch confronts his wife, Isobel, but what the authorities don't realise is that it's all a ruse enabling them to spend a weekend together.

WHAT A SCENE!

It's locking-up time at the prison and Barrowclough has a final word with Fletcher.

BARROWCLOUGH
You know, Fletcher, this is the part of the job I hate, you know, locking men up, caging them in.

FLETCHER
Yeah, 'tis a pity, too, just when the good telly is starting and all. It's a shame, ain't it? All we ever see is the news, ain't it? News and Nationwide. What's the good of Nationwide when you're stuck in here, eh?

BARROWCLOUGH
No, I've never got used to bolting these doors, you know. I think of all of you locked in these little cells and I . . . I think of me going out of here and . . . going home to my little house and my wife, who's waiting for me. (He looks forlorn)

FLETCHER
What's the matter, Mr Barrowclough?

BARROWCLOUGH
I sometimes wish I was in here with you lot!

SERIES TWO JUST DESSERTS

Original transmission: **Friday 24 October 1975**
BBC1, 8.30 p.m.

CAST

Norman Fletcher . . . . **Ronnie Barker**
Mr Barrowclough . . . . **Brian Wilde**
Mr Mackay . . . . **Fulton Mackay**
Lennie Godber . . . . **Richard Beckinsale**
Ives . . . . **Ken Jones**
Warren . . . . **Sam Kelly**
McLaren . . . . **Tony Osoba**
Lukewarm . . . . **Christopher Biggins**
Banyard . . . . **Eric Dodson**
Mr Appleton . . . . **Graham Ashley**
Mr Birchwood . . . . **John Rudling**
Gay Gordon . . . . **Felix Bowness**

There's a thief inside Slade Prison and Fletcher's disgusted. It
may be acceptable outside but pilfering from fellow lags is
inexcusable, especially as Fletch becomes the latest victim
when his tin of pineapple chunks (acquired courtesy of
Slade's kitchen) is swiped.

Fletcher holds an inquiry, but the meeting is broken up by
the prowling Mackay who disbelieves Fletch's lame explana-
tion that it's a gathering of the newly formed Slade Prison
Cowboy Club.

After losing his chunks, Fletcher realises his trust has
been misplaced and that prison is a 'jungle'; it's time he
concentrated on looking after number one. Later, Mr
Barrowclough informs Fletch he has found the tin of
chunks while conducting a random security check; he
knows it was stolen from the kitchen but won't report it so
long as Fletch keeps his nose clean. When it's discovered
that Mrs Barrowclough has eaten the chunks by mistake,
they formulate a plan to replace the tin . . . but it runs
anything but smoothly.

WHAT A SCENE!

Mackay is talking to Fletch about the increase in pilfering when Godber arrives dressed in his kitchen uniform.

MACKAY
This is a very unfortunate combination, isn't it?

FLETCHER
I dunno, sir.

MACKAY
Godber with his opportunities to steal from the kitchen and you with your distribution network.

GODBER
'Ere, I don't steal. I resent that.

MACKAY
Oh, you resent that, do you? I suppose butter wouldn't melt in your mouth?

FLETCHER
(Sarcastically) 'Ere that's a good idea, how much could you get in your mouth?

HEARTBREAK HOTEL

Original transmission: **Friday 31 October 1975**
BBC1, 8.30 p.m.

CAST

Norman Fletcher . . . . **Ronnie Barker**
Mr Barrowclough . . . . **Brian Wilde**
Mr Mackay . . . . **Fulton Mackay**
Lennie Godber . . . . **Richard Beckinsale**
Ingrid . . . . **Patricia Brake**
Mrs Godber . . . . **Maggie Flint**

Fletch is shocked to hear that Godber is up in front of the Governor after attacking Jackdaw with a soup ladle in the kitchen. Such irrational behaviour from one of Slade's more placid inmates takes everyone by surprise, but mitigating circumstances save him from a spell in the cooler.

Godber's bad news arrived in a letter from Denise, his fiancée, who announces in it that she's married someone else – a third engineer in the merchant navy called Kenneth. But Godber's bout of melancholia is short-lived when Fletcher's daughter, the bubbly Ingrid, appears on the scene.

WHAT A SCENE!

Mackay questions Fletch because six soft toilet rolls have disappeared from the Governor's personal toilet.

FLETCHER
Oh dear, would you adam and eve it, whatever next?

MACKAY
Knowing you, Fletcher, probably the seat.

(Godber laughs)

FLETCHER
Don't look at me, sir.

(Mackay turns to Godber)

GODBER
Nor me, it's writing paper I'm short of.

MACKAY
Well it's not right. We've had to give the Governor standard prison-issue tissue.

GODBER
That's rough.

FLETCHER
Rough? I'd say it is. That'll wipe the smile off his face.

Original transmission: 📺 **Friday 7 November 1975**
BBC1, 8.30 p.m.

CAST

Norman Fletcher . . . . **Ronnie Barker**
Mr Barrowclough . . . . **Brian Wilde**
Mr Mackay . . . . **Fulton Mackay**
Lennie Godber . . . . **Richard Beckinsale**
Mr Wainwright . . . . **Peter Jeffrey**
Williams . . . . **Philip Madoc**
Warren . . . . **Sam Kelly**
McLaren . . . . **Tony Osoba**
The Governor . . . . **Michael Barrington**
Secretary (Mrs Heskith) . . . . **Madge Hindle**

When the cat's away the mice will play, so with Mackay
attending a course, the prisoners plan working a few fiddles –
it's even suggested they could restart frog racing. But their
hopes are quickly dashed when Mackay's replacement turns
out to be the acid-tongued bully Wainwright, whom Fletcher
had the displeasure of meeting at Brixton. It's not long before
he's making his presence felt by curtailing the hours prisoners
can watch TV, banning talking in the exercise area and
removing the prisoners' ping-pong table; he even classes
Barrowclough as unfit to work anywhere except the prison
farm.

It's time action was taken against Wainwright's dictato-
rial behaviour and a riot is staged in the dining room. The
warders fail to regain control but when Fletcher tells the
Governor that Wainwright has inflamed the problem – and
that the only person who can quell the riot is
Barrowclough – the mild-mannered warder is brought in
from the cold.

WHAT A SCENE!

Barrowclough and Fletch discuss the ping-pong table, which has been moved to the warders' mess.

BARROWCLOUGH
Yes, well that's only till our billiard table is re-covered, you see.

FLETCHER
Oh yeah, well, yeah.

BARROWCLOUGH
Well, it was your fault it wanted re-covering.

FLETCHER
Our fault?

BARROWCLOUGH
Well some prisoner certainly tampered with it.

FLETCHER
Can you prove that?

BARROWCLOUGH
Well, we can surmise it. When Nosher Garrett went over the wall he was picked up in Blackpool wearing a green baize suit!

Original transmission: ▯ **Friday 14 November 1975
BBC1, 8.30 p.m.**

CAST

Norman Fletcher	**Ronnie Barker**
Mr Barrowclough	**Brian Wilde**
Mr Mackay	**Fulton Mackay**
Blanco	**David Jason**
Warren	**Sam Kelly**
McLaren	**Tony Osoba**
Banyard . . .	**Eric Dodson**
The Governor	**Michael Barrington**
Mr Collinson	**Paul McDowell**
Vicar	**Tony Aitken**
Prison Visitors	**Ivor Roberts**
. . . .	**Barbara New**
. . . .	**Geoffrey Greenhill**

It's Saturday afternoon and, while everyone is out in the fresh
air playing football, or down in the hobbies room, Fletch is
relaxing on his bunk reading a dirty magazine. Several people
ask him to play football, or join the prison's amateur
dramatic society: no one believes that all Fletch wants is to
be left alone. By the time Blanco arrives, Fletch has had
enough and decides to stretch his legs by wandering down to
Mr Collinson's office and stealing a couple of his Jaffa
Cakes.

Later, as he's settling down again, Barrowclough pops in
and they end up discussing prison life around the world,
before Mackay and three Home Office officials arrive.
However, the prison chaplain coming around is the final
straw and Fletch throws him over the balcony. The Governor
sentences him to three days in isolation, but Fletch is disappointed and pleads for more.

WHAT A SCENE!

Fletch and Barrowclough discuss the prison system abroad. Fletch wishes Slade would allow wives to stay.

FLETCHER
They have special apartments, you see, where the wife comes to stay the weekend, and then you spend the whole time manifesting your long-felt want.

BARROWCLOUGH
I don't know of any prison where . . .

FLETCHER
Maybe not here but certainly in Holland and also, I believe, in America, where they have a more enlightened penal system anyway.

BARROWCLOUGH
(Shocked) You mean the wives just visit and spend the whole weekend . . .

FLETCHER
Conjugating, yeah.

BARROWCLOUGH
That's more than I'm allowed at home!

SERIES TWO HAPPY RELEASE

Original transmission: 📺 **Friday 21 November 1975**
BBC1, 8.30 p.m.

CAST

Norman Fletcher . . . . **Ronnie Barker**
Mr Barrowclough . . . . **Brian Wilde**
Mr Mackay . . . . **Fulton Mackay**
Lennie Godber . . . . **Richard Beckinsale**
Blanco . . . . **David Jason**
Norris . . . . **Colin Farrell**
Mr Collinson . . . . **Paul McDowell**
Medical Officer . . . . **Terence Soall**

After the Carlisle General Hospital confirms that Fletcher has broken his ankle, he spends three weeks in the prison infirmary – a fact that angers Mackay. Fletch shares the ward with Blanco and the unlikeable Norris. When he learns that Norris has diddled the aged Blanco of his worldly goods during a card game, he devises a plan to reclaim his friend's possessions.

The crafty scheme seems to be working when Norris, on the eve of his release, overhears Blanco telling Fletch he's buried thousands of pounds in Leeds. Desperate to get his grubby little hands on the location map, he returns Blanco's possessions in exchange. But he's arrested before long for digging a hole in the middle of a football pitch!

WHAT A SCENE!

Blanco and Fletch are both in the prison infirmary, and the old man wakes up Fletch to tell him something, but all Fletcher wants to do is sleep.

BLANCO

There were three of us. We'd done a job on a wages van on its way to a fridge factory near Otley. Do you remember reading about it?

PORRIDGE

FLETCHER

No, I don't, no.

BLANCO

Well it was all in the Yorkshire Post.

FLETCHER

Yeah, well unless it made the Muswell Hill Standard or Titbits I'd have missed it.

BLANCO

Suppose so. Anyway it was an untidy job, a lot of things went wrong.

FLETCHER

Yeah, well you wouldn't be in here if it hadn't, would you?

BLANCO

No, no. Now the other two lads, they were brothers. There was Jack Barrett and Harry . . . (He can't remember the name)

FLETCHER

Barrett, was it?

BLANCO

That's right, did you know him?

FLETCHER

No, only through his brother, like.

BLANCO

'Cause you see, their escape was in the Yorkshire Post and all; they got away in a fishing boat from Bridlington.

FLETCHER

Yes, is this going to take long, Blanco, only my foot's gone to sleep and I'd like to catch it up, know what I mean?

Original transmission: **Friday 28 November 1975**
BBC1, 8.30 p.m.

CAST

Norman Fletcher . . . . **Ronnie Barker**
Mr Barrowclough . . . . **Brian Wilde**
Mr Mackay . . . . **Fulton Mackay**
Lennie Godber . . . . **Richard Beckinsale**
Harry Grout . . . . **Peter Vaughan**
Jackdaw . . . . **Cyril Shaps**
PTI . . . . **Roy Sampson**

Godber's chuffed when he's chosen for the boxing team, but Grouty is more excited because sport means betting. Keen to earn some cash, he asks Fletcher to study the form. Fletch reports that Godber looks a firm favourite for his bout and Grouty tells him to fix the fight so that he falls in the second round, thus ensuring Grouty wins a packet from his opponent, Nesbitt. Fletcher realises he's got a problem when Godber announces he's already promised Billy Moffat he'll go down in the first. A change of plan finds Fletcher trying to nobble Nesbitt and making Godber win . . . so what happens when both fighters hit the canvas?

WHAT A SCENE!

Fletch tells Mackay and Godber about an old friend who used to be a boxer.

FLETCHER
Well, I don't reckon boxing is such a noble art, anyway.

MACKAY
No, of course you wouldn't.

FLETCHER
No. I haven't told you this: I had a friend once, he was a

---

good boy, he was, light-heavy, you know, good strong lad. He won a few fights. Then, of course, he thought he was the bee's knees, didn't he, hey? Fast cars, loose women. Classic story: too much too soon; he just blew up, got into debt. Do you know where he finished up? In a boxing booth in a fairground. Four fights a night, seven nights a week. Well, the body can't take that sort of punishment, can it? The brain just went soft, reflexes went, got punchy. He just became a vegetable, an incoherent, non-thinking zombie.

MACKAY
What became of him?

FLETCHER
He joined the prison service as a warder. He's doing very well.

Original transmission: **Wednesday 24 December 1975**
BBC1, 8.25 p.m.

CAST

Norman Fletcher . . . . **Ronnie Barker**
Mr Barrowclough . . . . **Brian Wilde**
Mr Mackay . . . . **Fulton Mackay**
Lennie Godber . . . . **Richard Beckinsale**
Harry Grout . . . . **Peter Vaughan**
Prison Doctor . . . . **Graham Crowden**
Warren . . . . **Sam Kelly**
Lukewarm . . . . **Christopher Biggins**
Sandra . . . . **Carol Hawkins**
Nurse . . . . **Elisabeth Day**

Slade's Godfather, Harry Grout, is helping fellow inmate
Tommy Slocombe tunnel his way to freedom in time for
Christmas – and he expects everyone to pull their weight. But
Fletch thinks it's bad news, because if he succeeds everyone else
will suffer.

To wriggle his way out of helping, he feigns injury in an
attempt to get hospitalised for the duration of the festive
period. But relying on his old cartilage trouble doesn't
convince the prison doctor, proud of his infirmary's low
admission record, to give him a bed. Insisting that he be
taken seriously, Fletcher is referred to a civilian hospital for
examination.

News of Fletch's trip outside is music to Grouty's ears,
and he forces him into collecting an important package
containing a blank passport for Slocombe. The X-rays reveal
a healthy knee, but just before Fletch leaves hospital a nurse
hands him the secret package.

A relieved Fletcher hands over the passport upon his
return to Slade Prison. Just when he thinks his good deeds
are complete, however, he's given another job – one that
results in him being hospitalised after all.

111

WHAT A SCENE!

Fletch discusses with Godber the benefits of Slade Prison's Christmas tree.

GODBER
We've got such a lot to look forward to: concert coming up, and the carol service – and the tree.

FLETCHER
Yeah, very useful that tree.

GODBER
Useful?

FLETCHER
Yeah, for stashing Christmas contraband. All them dingly-danglies hide a multitude of sins, you know. Even the fairy on the top's got two ounces of tobacco stuffed up her tutu!

GODBER
(Smiling) No wonder she looks uncomfortable.

Original transmission: 📺 **Friday 24 December 1976**
BBC1, 8 p.m.

CAST

Norman Fletcher	**Ronnie Barker**
Mr Barrowclough	**Brian Wilde**
Mr Mackay	**Fulton Mackay**
Lennie Godber	**Richard Beckinsale**
Reg Urwin	**Dudley Sutton**
Warren	**Sam Kelly**
McLaren	**Tony Osoba**
The Governor	**Michael Barrington**
Keegan	**Ken Wynne**
Tulip	**Michael Redfern**
Mrs Jamieson	**Jane Wenham**

Unbeknown to everyone, Fletcher and Godber have been fermenting illicit liquor for months and it's reaching maturity just in time for the festive season. Meanwhile, the Governor hates Christmas time inside and prays that the period will pass peacefully. But no such luck – Mackay catches Fletcher and Godber, red-handed, indulging in their booze.

They're marched off to the Governor's office but while they're waiting, Reg Urwin – who's replaced Keegan as the Governor's tea boy – pops in. Finding Barrowclough alone in the office, he seizes his opportunity and takes the warder hostage, demanding ten grand and a helicopter or else he won't be responsible for his actions.

A plan is hatched to resolve the problem and Mackay, who's banished from the office, returns with cups of coffee, one laced with a tranquilliser. But Fletcher is mistakenly handed the cup and before long is fast asleep. Upon recovering, a newscaster on the radio states that three prisoners are involved in the incident. Annoyed that he's been implicated, Fletch decides it's time to persuade Urwin to give himself up.

WHAT A SCENE!

Fletch asks some of his inmates about the real meaning of Christmas.

GODBER

Chestnuts roasting on an open fire.

FLETCHER

Yeah, yeah, yeah, very good, yeah.

MCLAREN

Hey, what about Mr Mackay roasting on an open fire?

FLETCHER

(Laughs) That's Guy Fawkes' Night.

Original transmission: **Friday 18 February 1977**
BBC1, 8.30 p.m.

CAST

Norman Fletcher	**Ronnie Barker**
Mr Barrowclough	**Brian Wilde**
Mr Mackay	**Fulton Mackay**
Lennie Godber	**Richard Beckinsale**
Harry Grout	**Peter Vaughan**
Harris	**Ronald Lacey**
Warren	**Sam Kelly**
McLaren	**Tony Osoba**
Lukewarm	**Christopher Biggins**
Spider	**John Moore**
Crusher	**John Dair**

While Fletcher enjoys a cuppa in the recreation area, Mackay searches Harris on the landing, suspecting him of pinching pills from the medical room. But before Mackay discovers them, the bottle drops into the unsuspecting Fletcher's mug of tea.

When Grouty discovers pills have been nabbed he demands Fletcher's help: if they're not returned to the medical room within the hour, Mackay will order a thorough stock-take, exposing Grouty's lucrative drug-peddling business in the process. With Fletcher working in the admin block, Grouty feels he could whip some pills from one of the women workers to replace the stolen pack.

A little arm-twisting saves the day for Fletch and he secures some replacement tablets in time, but before the evening is out he discovers the bottle that fell into his mug. With Mackay on the warpath, there's no alternative but to swallow the evidence.

WHAT A SCENE!

Warren disturbs Fletcher.

WARREN
What are you reading, Fletch?

FLETCHER
(Looks at his novel) A book.

WARREN
No, I mean what sort of book?

FLETCHER
Paperback sort of book, you know the sort of thing: lots of bits of paper all stuck down together, down the left-hand side.

WARREN
Is it a good book?

FLETCHER
Dunno until I finish it, do I? It might turn out rotten in the end. I shan't finish it, either, if I get these continuing interruptions, shall I?

WARREN
I'd read books if I could read. Is it a dirty book?

FLETCHER
Yeah, filthy, dropped it in a puddle coming back from lunch.

Original transmission: 📺 **Friday 25 February 1977**
BBC1, 8.30 p.m.

CAST

Norman Fletcher	**Ronnie Barker**
Mr Barrowclough	**Brian Wilde**
Mr Mackay	**Fulton Mackay**
Lennie Godber	**Richard Beckinsale**
Rawley	**Maurice Denham**
Harris	**Ronald Lacey**
Warren	**Sam Kelly**
McLaren	**Tony Osoba**
The Governor	**Michael Barrington**
Mr Collinson	**Paul McDowell**

Fletch goes bananas when he discovers he'll have to share his cell with a third inmate. But he feels even worse when the new arrival turns out to be Rawley, a close friend of the Governor's and, more shockingly, the judge who sentenced Fletcher. Fletch regards the judge as representing the establishment – and soon puts him in his place when he catches Godber making Rawley's bed.

As the cell door slams at the end of his first day inside, Rawley is suddenly aware of what prison life is like. Adjusting to his new surroundings isn't easy for a man who's enjoyed the finer things in life; before the episode closes, he faces being beaten up – until Fletcher intervenes.

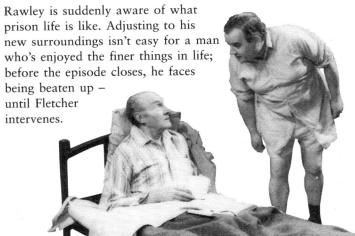

WHAT A SCENE!

Godber and Harris move a new bed into Fletcher's cell.

GODBER

Fletcher's not going to like this, Mr Barrowclough.

HARRIS

He naffing won't.

(Looking at Godber)

He didn't like you moving in, let alone a third.

BARROWCLOUGH

Fletcher will have no choice in the matter; we're running a prison not a hotel. Prisons are very overcrowded this time of year.

GODBER

Not surprising, it's bitter out.

Original transmission: Friday 4 March 1977
BBC1, 8.30 p.m.

CAST

Norman Fletcher	**Ronnie Barker**
Mr Barrowclough	**Brian Wilde**
Mr Mackay	**Fulton Mackay**
Lennie Godber	**Richard Beckinsale**
Rawley	**Maurice Denham**
Harris	**Ronald Lacey**
Warren	**Sam Kelly**
McLaren	**Tony Osoba**

While Rawley awaits his appeal, Fletcher presents him with a business proposition: he suggests dishing out legal advice to fellow prisoners in a partnership which would entail Fletch securing the trade and the judge imparting his knowledge. Rawley, however, isn't interested.

Fletch might have warmed a little towards his new cell-mate, but not everyone feels the same. Harris especially is unsympathetic, having been relegated to swilling pigs while Rawley ends up with a cushy clerical job. So when the judge's watch goes missing, Harris is chief suspect. To resolve the matter, Fletch calls a special court hearing with Rawley reluctantly presiding over the case.

It's not long until the case is dismissed due to lack of evidence, but it's surprising what a little arm-twisting, courtesy of McLaren, can do: before long, Harris has confessed and returned the watch.

There is more good news for Rawley: he wins his appeal and leaves Slade Prison, stating that he'll do whatever he can to improve the prison system.

WHAT A SCENE!

Warren asks Fletch to write him a letter.

FLETCHER
Don't you think you could have taken advantage of the educational facilities in 'ere and cured your illiteracy?

WARREN
I'm not illiterate, Fletch.

FLETCHER
Oh, I'm sorry. I thought that was the word we used for people who can't read or write.

WARREN
I'm not illiterate. I suffer from dyslexia. (Fletch looks puzzled) You don't know what it means, do ya?

FLETCHER
Well, obviously it's got to be some sort of acid stomach, hasn't it? But why that should stop you reading and writing I cannot imagine.

WARREN
No, no, you're wrong, dyslexia is word blindness, like. I can't make out words when they're written down, you see, they all get jumbled up in my head.

FLETCHER
Well, plenty of room, isn't there?

Original transmission: **Friday 11 March 1977**
BBC1, 8.30 p.m.

CAST

Norman Fletcher . . . . **Ronnie Barker**
Mr Barrowclough . . . . **Brian Wilde**
Mr Mackay . . . . **Fulton Mackay**
Lennie Godber . . . . **Richard Beckinsale**
Blanco . . . . **David Jason**

When old-timer Blanco's parole is granted, Lukewarm, Godber and Fletcher's congratulations are short-lived when Blanco protests his innocence and refuses parole – fearing he'd be admitting guilt for his crime.

To help their old inmate retain his pride as well as his freedom, Fletch, Lukewarm and Godber launch CROW (Campaign for the Release of Old Webb). Their campaign has two objectives: to demand a retrial, or to force the Governor to ask the Home Office for a pardon. To draw attention to their crusade Fletch informs Mr Venables that Blanco is considering a hunger strike; the last thing the Governor needs in Slade Prison is a martyr.

To save face and avoid any nasty publicity, Venables drops the Home Office a line and soon Blanco is awarded a pardon. But he's not as innocent as he looks.

WHAT A SCENE!

Fletch, Lukewarm, Blanco and Godber discuss what they were doing in 1959, the year Blanco was imprisoned.

GODBER
I was in junior school in 1959. Sat next to Ann Podmore; she was left-handed.

FLETCHER
(Turning to Lukewarm) Fascinating. I bet he got on the right side of her!

Original transmission: Friday 18 March 1977
BBC1, 8.30 p.m.

CAST

Norman Fletcher	**Ronnie Barker**
Mr Barrowclough	**Brian Wilde**
Mr Mackay	**Fulton Mackay**
Lennie Godber	**Richard Beckinsale**
Spraggon	**Alun Armstrong**
Warren	**Sam Kelly**
McLaren	**Tony Osoba**

Godber's swotting for his history O level, but he's finding it tough thanks to constant interruptions from the likes of Fletcher and Warren. When he storms out of the cell, Fletch and Warren realise how much the exam means to him – and that failure might send him back to crime upon his impending release. To help their friend pass the O level, they steal the exam paper.

But Godber doesn't want anything to do with it; he feels he's cheated all his life and wants to pass through his own merits – just as well, because the illiterate Warren has nicked the biology papers by mistake!

WHAT A SCENE!

Mackay tells Fletcher and Godber about his hard childhood.

MACKAY

I had to leave school at fourteen to help bring a living wage into the house – hard times on those Lanarkshire coal fields. My father was an unemployed miner, but there were still eight children to provide for.

FLETCHER

Oh, eight kids, eh. He wasn't unemployed the whole of the time, then?

Original transmission: 📺 **Friday 25 March 1977**
BBC1, 8.30 p.m.

CAST

Norman Fletcher	**Ronnie Barker**
Mr Barrowclough	**Brian Wilde**
Mr Mackay	**Fulton Mackay**
Lennie Godber	**Richard Beckinsale**
Jarvis	**David Daker**
Warren	**Sam Kelly**
Ingrid	**Patricia Brake**
Crusher	**John Dair**

Godber is up for parole soon and, as Fletch tells Ingrid, who's become his pen pal, his 'boyhood charm' will see him through. But he jeopardises his prospects when he's offended by remarks made by tough-nut Jarvis and starts a brawl. Even Fletcher's advice to steer clear of the Mancunian thug falls on deaf ears as Godber insists that 'a man's got to do what a man's got to do' – even if it means kissing goodbye to freedom.

Desperate to help his cellmate, Fletch discusses with Warren what they can do. After chewing over several ideas, including using drugs from the prison farm to tranquillise Jarvis, there seems only one option: Fletch will have to confront Jarvis himself, even if it means blotting his own copybook. Any aggro should result in Jarvis being locked away until after the parole hearing. Fletch, however, finds it hard getting the reaction he wants from Jarvis; but then Crusher unwittingly saves the day.

Godber's parole is granted and in an emotional final scene he thanks Fletcher for all his help. Then he breaks the news that he's got a new sweetheart: Ingrid!

WHAT A SCENE!

Ingrid visits Fletch and they discuss Marion, who he feels is lazy.

FLETCHER

Does she still work in Woolworths?

INGRID

No, not now, she don't need to, Dad. Her boyfriend, Ricky, is ever so well off. He's got three cars. He gave her one for Christmas.

FLETCHER

Yeah, I bet he did. Did she get a present as well?

INGRID

Dad! If she marries Ricky she'll want for nothing.

FLETCHER

If. What does he do?

INGRID

He runs these cheap charter aeroplane-trips.

FLETCHER

Oh yeah, what are they called: Gullible's Travels?

ALL EPISODES WRITTEN BY
Dick Clement and Ian La Frenais

MUSIC
Max Harris

FILM CAMERAMEN
Len Newson (S1/episodes 1–3 & 6); Keith Taylor (S1/episodes 4–5);
Ken Willicombe (S2/episodes 2–4 & 6); Kenneth MacMillan (S2/episode 5);
John Tiley ('No Way Out'); John McGlashan (S3)

FILM EDITORS
Geoffrey Botterill (S1/episodes 1–2); Ray Millichope (S1/episodes 3–6;
S2/episodes 2–6;
'No Way Out'); John Dunstan (S3)

FILM SOUND
Ron Blight (credited on 'No Way Out')

MAKE-UP
Sylvia James (S1); Ann Ailes-Stevenson (S2; 'No Way Out');
Suzanne Broad ('The Desperate Hours'; S3)

COSTUMES
Mary Husband (S1; S3); Betty Aldiss (S2); Susan Wheal ('No Way Out');
Robin Stubbs ('The Desperate Hours')

LIGHTING
Peter Smee (S1/episodes 1–4 & 6; S2/episodes 1–4; 'No Way Out'); Peter
Wesson (S1/episode 5; S3);
Brian Clemett (S2/episode 5); Sam Barclay ('The Desperate Hours')

SOUND
Anthony Philpot (S1; S2; 'The Desperate Hours'); Jeff Booth ('No Way
Out'); John Holmes (S3)

PRODUCTION ASSISTANT
Ray Butt (S1); Dave Perrottet (S2); Alan Bell ('No Way Out'); Mike Crisp
('The Desperate Hours'; S3)

TECHNICAL ADVISER
Jonathan Marshall (credited on S1/episodes 1–4)

DESIGNER
Tim Gleeson (S1/episodes 1–2 & 5–6; S2/episode 1; 'No Way Out'; 'The
Desperate Hours'; S3);
David Chandler (S1/episodes 3 & 6); Gerry Scott (S1/episodes 4–5); John
Pusey (S2/episodes 2–6)

PRODUCER/DIRECTOR
Sydney Lotterby

MEET THE OTHER INMATES

Banyard

Banyard – who teaches chess at Slade – appeared in two episodes, 'Just Desserts' and 'No Peace for the Wicked', as a disgraced dentist. He regards himself as superior to other prisoners, not a 'common criminal', an attitude which nettles fellow inmates – especially because he's serving time for 'mistreating' women after putting them under laughing gas!

Banyard was played by Eric Dodson, who was born in Peterborough in 1920 and started amateur acting while waiting for his call-up during World War II. He eventually joined the RAF in 1941 and trained in Canada in coastal command before spending the rest of the war flying bombers and, in 1944, serving in Yugoslavia as a liaison officer.

When he was demobbed he returned to acting, initially in rep in Edinburgh. After spending several years working the repertory circuit, he made his West End debut in *The Young Elizabeth* in the early 1950s.

He also appeared in various films, including *Night Train for Inverness* (1960), *Sentenced for Life* (1960), *The Dock Brief* (1962), *Battle of Britain* (1969), *The Mirror Crack'd* (1980), with Elizabeth Taylor, and *The Walter Ego* (1991).

On television, he was seen as the head porter in *Jekyll and Hyde*, Sir Gerald in *Suspicion*, Reverend Johns in *Poldark*, a magistrate in *Lovejoy*, Sir Robert in *Grace and Favour*, Sir Edward in *Press Gang*, and as a village headman in *Doctor Who*. He also appeared in *The Sweeney, The Saint, The Avengers, Fresh Fields, Rumpole of the Bailey, All Creatures Great and Small, It Ain't Half Hot, Mum* and *'Allo, 'Allo*.

A long illness prevented Eric from working for the last five years of his life, and he died in January 2000.

Crusher

The almighty Crusher is one of Harry Grout's henchmen, and he's summoned whenever some muscle is required.

John Dair was topping the bill as a singer at London's Lyceum when he was offered the chance to play Crusher in the series. 'A gentleman called Cliff Castle from the BBC asked me one night if I'd ever thought of doing television. I thought he was referring to my voice, but a week later he phoned and asked if I fancied doing a bit on *Porridge*. I initially appeared in the episode 'The Harder They Fall', the first television job I ever had.'

Unfortunately the costume department at the Beeb couldn't find a prison suit big enough to fit John's large frame. 'I used to wear a boiler suit. After finishing the boxing-match scenes on location, I noticed Ronnie Barker and the director looking at me; I thought they were going to throw me off because I didn't have a prison suit, but they asked if I'd come back on Sunday to do some filming in front of the audience. From there, I returned to appear in several other episodes.'

John, who's now seventy, saw his character as a 'heavy' and thus his presence his most important feature. 'I must have done all right, because I then became Crusher. And in the film I was known as Samson, who had a head-case of a mate – a psychopath called Delilah. It was a fantastic time, working on *Porridge*.'

Thanks to the exposure he received on the sitcom, John Dair never looked back. He went on to appear on numerous shows, including *The Ken Dodd Show, The Morecambe and Wise Show, Jack the Ripper, Our Friends in the North* – in which he played Charlie Dawson – and an episode of *The Lenny Henry Show*, as Father Christmas. On the big screen, he appeared as Big John in 1983's *Yellowbeard*, Vinnie Ricorso in *Batman* (1989), the Fat Man in *Sweet Nothing* (1990), Derek in *Hear My Song* (1991) and Macleish in *Loch Ness* (1995).

Born in Dundee, John drove bulldozers and mobile cranes on building sites before turning to singing. At a club one evening, he happened to mention that he could sing better than the entertainer could and was invited on stage to prove it. He sang two songs and before the night was out received various invites to sing in local clubs. He travelled the country before working at the Strand for four years.

John no longer sings professionally and concentrates on acting instead; he's also been seen in commercials, including a recent one for Wall's sausages.

Dylan

Dylan – real name Melvin Bottomley – is a hippie who in 'A Day Out' joins the working party assigned the task of helping the local council dig drainage ditches. Described by Fletch as 'lazy', Dylan was thrown out of art school for drawing on the walls and is one of Slade's eccentrics – he wears an earring, his hair is long and he tiedyes his uniform.

Philip Jackson enjoyed the experience of appearing as Dylan in *Porridge*, but avoids watching the episode like the plague. 'It's not a pleasant experience, watching myself; I look very inexperienced in the episode, like I'm on automatic pilot. And, of course, in hindsight you always notice things you'd have done differently, given the chance to do the job again.'

Born in Retford, Nottinghamshire, in 1948, Philip gained a BA in drama from Bristol University. He'd acted as a child at school and youth clubs, but when he embarked on his degree course he envisaged becoming a director rather than an actor. However, further forays on the stage during his student days saw him head for an acting career, beginning at the Liverpool Playhouse as a soldier in *Coriolanus*. Philip remained at Liverpool for eighteen months before striking lucky and working with The Royal Court.

Philip was appearing in *Blooming Youth* for the BBC when Syd Lotterby saw him. Shortly afterwards, he was offered the role of Dylan. His extensive small-screen CV includes appearances in *Coronation Street, Murder Most Horrid, Hamish Macbeth, Heartbeat, Coming Home, Last of the Summer Wine* (as Gordon), *Touching Evil* and *The Last Salute*, as Leonard Spanwick. He's also worked on several films.

Philip last worked in the theatre seven years ago, and nowadays the medium of television dominates his time. He recently played Robert in the series *Black Cab* and Chief Inspector Japp in episodes of *Poirot*.

Evans

Evans is first mentioned by Mackay in 'New Faces, Old Hands', but is not actually seen until the second episode in series one, 'The Hustler'. Mackay informs the Governor that Evans had to be isolated for attempting to eat electric light-bulbs upon discovering he couldn't get any razor blades, so you can imagine Fletch's reaction when he discovers he's got to share a cell with him! The Welshman is rarely seen without his cap or obligatory fag clinging to his lower lip – even during regular visits to the psychiatrist.

Ray Dunbobbin, who during his career saw success as both writer and actor, played Evans. Born in Canada, Ray moved to Liverpool with his British parents as a boy. He completed his education in the city and upon leaving school furthered his interest in art by working in a couple of Liverpool's art studios.

By this point in his life, Ray had developed an enthusiasm for acting and spent much of his spare time performing with a local amateur dramatics society. During a performance one evening, he was spotted and offered a chance to double for film actor Sam Kydd for a picture being shot at nearby Birkenhead. Ray went on to appear in numerous other films as well as establishing himself on television – often playing older characters. He was seen as a photographer in *Bergerac*, as Mr Boswell in five series of *The Liver Birds*, in *Doctor Who, Last of the Summer Wine, I Didn't Know You Cared* and *Hallelujah!* But people will probably remember him most for the six and a half years he spent playing Ralph Hardwicke in *Brookside*.

His busy career saw him appear in more than 500 radio and TV programmes. However, there were many other facets to Ray's career: alongside his acting, he became a successful scriptwriter for radio, stage and television (he scripted several episodes of *Z Cars* as well as drama and suspense plays for the BBC and Spanish television) and was a professional after-dinner speaker. For a while, Ray worked for a leading spoken-word cassette-company, abridging novels and acting as narrator.

A multitalented performer, Ray died of a heart attack in 1998.

Gay Gordon

Gay Gordon, who wears his hair in curlers, is first seen in 'Just Desserts'. Little is known about the prison poof other than that he's an oddball character with whom you wouldn't want to be stuck in a lift!

Playing the effeminate inmate was Felix Bowness. Born in Harwell and an amateur-boxing champion in his late teens, Felix has been in the entertainment business for more than four decades performing in variety shows around the country. A veteran warm-up man, he won a talent contest in Reading that led to him turning semi-pro. Then, while working in cabaret, he was spotted by a BBC producer and given a small part in radio.

With great tenacity, Felix kept plugging away, eventually making his TV debut as a stand-up comic before moving into comedy roles in shows like *Dad's Army* (in which he played three different parts).

Felix is perhaps best known for his role as jockey Fred Quilley in *Hi-De-Hi!*, and has worked frequently for the writing partnership of Jimmy Perry and David Croft: he was a customer in *Are You Being Served?*, a grocer in *You Rang,*

M'Lord?, and appeared in the earlier series *Hugh and I*. He played a relief guard in the series *Oh, Doctor Beeching!*, as well as warming up the audiences prior to recordings.

Harry Grout

Harry Grout is the Godfather of Slade Prison. He leads a comparatively cushy life as he moves towards his release; while everyone else works, he's in charge of the prison's swimming pool – even though there isn't one. Grouty is a highly influential figure – partly due to his bully-boy tactics – who served time at Parkhurst where he owned a pigeon, thus enabling him to keep in touch with his bookies. While those around him endure their Spartan lifestyle, he lives in relative luxury thanks to his radio and cigars, the company of his pet budgie (Seymour), and his pull with the warders, who bend over backwards to help him.

Harry was played by Peter Vaughan, who started his career as an ASM in repertory theatre. Born in Wem, Shropshire, in 1924, Peter has worked extensively in the theatre and on screen. His film credits include: *Sapphire, Village of the Damned, Smokescreen* and, more recently, *Remains of the Day*. His television portfolio, meanwhile, covers shows such as *The Pallisers, The Persuaders, The Sweeney, The Adventurer, Randall and Hopkirk (Deceased), Crane, Man in a Suitcase, Adam Adamant Lives!, Citizen Smith, Great Expectations, Chancer, The Return of Sherlock Holmes, Murder Most Horrid, Lovejoy* and *Our Friends in the North* (playing Felix Hutchinson).

Harris

Greasy-haired Harris is an overgrown Teddy Boy who can't be trusted around Slade Prison. His slimy nature means he's not the most popular character behind bars, especially as he's serving time for trying to snatch an old-age pensioner's handbag (though he failed because the brave-hearted lady hit

him with her bag before pinning him down until the police arrived). As Fletch states: he's all 'wind and water'. Harris is an annoying moaner whose nose is put out of joint when he's relegated to pig-swilling upon Judge Rawley's arrival at Slade Prison.

The late Ronald Lacey, who played Harris, was born in Harrow in 1935. His early ambition was to become a professional sportsman, but he opted for acting instead and trained at a London drama school. After several years of repertory work, he made his movie debut in 1961's *The Boys*, playing Billy Herne.

The sixties also saw the start of his television career, with early appearances including episodes of *The Avengers* (1961), *Gideon's Way* (1965), *Out of the Unknown* (1965), *Randall and Hopkirk (Deceased)* (1969), *Department S* (1969) and several episodes as Ryland in *Jason King* (1971).

By the time his life was tragically cut short in 1991 by bowel cancer, Ronald, who also ran a theatrical agency, had built up an impressive list of credits encompassing the whole industry, including a spell on Broadway in *Chips With Everything*.

Other films he was seen in include: *Doctor in Distress, The Comedy Man, Catch Us If You Can, Dance of the Vampires, Say Hello to Yesterday, The Prince and the Pauper, The Death Angel* and *Yellowbeard*. While on the box he also appeared in shows like *The Sweeney, Blake's 7, Bergerac, Boon, Face to Face, Whatever Happened to the Likely Lads?* and *Minder on the Orient Express*.

Cyril Heslop

The brainless Cyril Heslop, who's also done bird at Shepton Mallet, arrives at Slade Prison the same time as Fletch and Godber. Aged forty-one, prisoner 8995 is on his third stretch of porridge, this time serving three years for robbery. Heslop is as thick as two short planks, is married to Iris and comes from Kent. He's seen in three episodes: 'New Faces, Old

Hands', 'The Hustler' and 'Men without Women', when he admits that his wife's sister, Gwendoline, who lives in Sidcup, attacked him in her kitchen and they ended up in bed.

Cast as Cyril Heslop was veteran actor Brian Glover. Born in Sheffield in 1934, Brian worked as a teacher and professional wrestler before turning to acting. A busy career saw this distinctive thespian appear in a host of shows, on stage and screen. Included in his television work are roles in *The Sweeney, Raffles, Target, Hazell* and *Doctor Who*. He also played Mr Dawson in *All Creatures Great and Small*, Mr Rottweiler in *Bottom*, Ken Farley in *The Bill*, and parts in *Don't Ask Me, The Secret Army, Return of the Saint* and *Minder* as well as Magersfontein Lugg in the 1989 series *Campion*.

On the big screen, Brian – who died in 1997 – worked on more than twenty films, including *Kes, O Lucky Man!, Brannigan, Trial by Combat, The First Great Train Robbery, An American Werewolf in London, Britannia Hospital, The Company of Wolves, Leon the Pig Farmer* and *Prince of Jutland*.

Ives

Ives, the man who everybody grew to hate, was an untrust-worthy know-all who infuriated his fellow prisoners. A scouser serving time for fraud, he's a lifelong cheat.

When Liverpudlian actor Ken Jones began playing Ives, life couldn't have been busier: he was also appearing as Rex in Eric Chappell's office comedy *The Squirrels* with Patsy Rowlands and Bernard Hepton. 'I used to do *Porridge* in the morning and *The Squirrels* in the afternoon. I played Ives for a few episodes in series two but became so busy I had to reluctantly give up *Porridge*.' Having to leave the sitcom saddened Ken. 'It's not often you come across quality material so I would've liked to have stayed, but it just wasn't feasible.'

Ken feels every episode of Clement and La Frenais' sitcom was like a 'little play'. 'They were beautifully constructed and the actual situation was fantastic: if you get a closed environment like a prison and an anarchist like Fletcher trying to break the system, there's wonderful conflict. The scripts were well written.'

Ken was born in Liverpool in 1930 and left school at fourteen, joining the building trade. He eventually also ran an amateur theatre in the city for four years, together with his wife, actress Sheila Fay, who was then working as a teacher. Some years later, they decided to try their luck as professionals and joined RADA together, graduating in 1960.

Ken's career got off to a flying start when he went straight into the West End as well as appearing in the first episode of *Z Cars* (in which he went on to play a semi-regular character, Felix Smithers, a police photographer). Alongside his small-screen career Ken continued to work a great deal in rep, including a spell with Joan Littlewood's Theatre Workshop. His TV credits include *United!*, *The Planemakers*, *Hunter's Walk*, *Go for Gold*, *The Liver Birds*, *Emmerdale Farm*, *Coronation Street*, *Watching*, *Goodnight Sweetheart*, *Peak Practice* and *The Detectives*.

Ken, who now lives in West Wales, continues to work and was recently seen in *Casualty* and other television projects.

Jackdaw

The wimpy Jackdaw acts as a runner for Grouty, and appeared in 'The Harder They Fall'.

Cyril Shaps played Jackdaw, the man who tells Fletch he's wanted by Harry Grout. Born in London in 1923, Cyril worked for the London County Council's ambulance service as a clerk for five years upon leaving school. When World War II broke out, he spent five years with the Service and Educational Corps. Before he returned to civvy street in 1947, Cyril – who had always wanted to be an actor – helped prepare soldiers for demob by teaching music and drama appreciation.

When he finally left the army he won a scholarship to RADA; after graduating, he secured his first post in rep at Guildford followed by a spell in the West End. For two years he worked on Holland's radio network where his range of duties was varied, including reporting, producing and announcing. He returned to England and struggled on the job front until the chance to join the BBC's own repertory company came along.

He gradually established himself on radio and television, appearing in various shows, such as *Z Cars* and *Doctor Who*. His first film role was in 1950's *Cario Road*, and other productions he worked on include: *The Silent Enemy; Danger Within; Passport to Shame; Never Let Go; Return of a Stranger; To Sir, With Love; The Odessa File; Operation Daybreak* and *The Spy Who Loved Me*. Cyril is still busy in the profession.

Reggie Jarvis

Mancunian Reggie Jarvis appeared in the closing episode, 'Final Stretch'. Nicknamed The Red Menace (he's a Manchester United supporter), the aggressive inmate has a foul temper – as exemplified by his smashing the prison television because he couldn't get a decent picture while watching his favourite programme, *The Magic Roundabout*. Within the same episode we also see him brawling with Godber, so it's clear he's the sort of guy worth avoiding at all costs.

Jarvis was played by busy character-actor David Daker, who has appeared in shows such as *Z Cars* (as P.C. Owen Culshaw), *Doctor Who*, *UFO*, *Strangers* (as Roy Stevens), *Juliet Bravo*, *Sorry!*, *Casualty*, *The Bill*, *Midsomer Murders*, *The Fallen Curtain*, *Crown Prosecutor* (as Ben Campbell), *Boon* and *The Woman in Black*.

Keegan

Keegan, who's seen in 'The Desperate Hours', is to be released shortly. Convicted for murdering his wife with poison, it seems odd that he's been allocated a job in the kitchen at Slade. When we get to see Keegan, he's become a trusty and serves the Governor his daily cuppas. However, Mr Venables can't ever come to terms with a murderer serving his tea and removes him from his duties – even though Mackay classes Keegan a 'model prisoner'.

Reading-born Ken Wynne played Keegan in the 1976 Christmas episode. Ken's father was a goods manager with Great Western Railways, which meant frequent relocations; despite those, most of his childhood was spent in Banbury.

He started acting with the Banbury County School and quickly reached the conclusion that he never wanted to do anything else with his life. Upon completing national service in the army, Ken set about realising his ambitions and was soon offered his first professional job at Stratford-upon-Avon in 1946, a venue he returned to many times during his career. His association with the Royal Shakespeare Company extended to a tour of Australia in 1953.

Ken has appeared in most of the West End theatres and has spent much of his acting life on the stage. He has nevertheless found time to grace the small screen in many programmes, including several episodes of *Dixon of Dock Green* – playing a policeman's nark – as the eccentric Mr Deacon in *The Fall and Rise of Reginald Perrin*, Reg Partridge in *Lovejoy*, Fenner in *The Sweeney*, Greasy Spriggs in *The Bounder*, the churlish farmer Dennis Pratt in *All Creatures Great and Small*, and as Ernie Mears in *EastEnders*.

His film credits, meanwhile, include *Decline and Fall of a Birdwatcher, Up Pompeii, The Alf Garnett Saga, Galileo* and *The Mystery of Edwin Drood*.

Lukewarm

Lukewarm, who works in the kitchen, originates from Middlesbrough and is described by Fletch as being 'lilac'. Within three months of Lukewarm's release, we hear from Fletcher that he's back in trouble after stealing a lady's handbag – though he claimed it was his own. A keen knitter, Lukewarm shares a cell with old-man Blanco, while his life outside is shared with Trevor, a watch repairer from Southport.

Oldham-born Christopher Biggins had no doubts about how to play Lukewarm. 'He was obviously an iron hoof – which is a wonderful term for poof – but none of us wanted him to be a mincing queen, so it was played, basically, a bit like me. For example, I used to do knitting so I suggested the character should knit, which helped make him a little fey.'

Lukewarm was one of the memorable inmates, and Christopher enjoyed being associated with the show. 'When we finished the first series, Ronnie gave the regulars a silver tankard with "Slade Prison, 1974" and our names inscribed on it. It was fantastic fun: not only was I working with a brilliant script, which is so important, but we also had Ronnie Barker who was generous to a fault. He's not a comedian, he's a comic actor of genius; and if he felt one of his lines was better said by me or somebody else, they would have it.

'It will always be a classic and its success is also due to Syd Lotterby, who managed to assemble the most wonderful cast. We had a lot of laughs doing it, and it was one of those jobs you enjoyed going to work for. There wasn't one dud performance in the whole of the series, and I'm very proud to have been involved.'

Christopher, who's also a director, grew up in Salisbury and attended elocution lessons while at school. His teacher introduced him to the theatre, and he joined the local rep. He had initially intended to stay just two weeks, but remained for two years – by the end of which time he'd earned his Equity card. Wishing to receive formal training, Christopher attended Bristol Old Vic Theatre School before joining Derby Rep. Not much later he made his West End debut in *The Owl and the Pussycat Went to Sea*, playing Head Jumbly.

His first role on TV was playing a thief in *Paul Temple*, but other credits include Podge in Clement and La Frenais' *Whatever Happened to the Likely Lads?*, Adam Painting in *Rentaghost*, Brian Reeves in the BBC sitcom *Watch This Space*, Nero in *I, Claudius*, a student in *Some Mothers Do 'Ave 'Em*, and work on *Upstairs, Downstairs, Five's Company, Poldark, Jackanory, Kidnapped* and *Surprise, Surprise*.

He's also appeared in a handful of films, including *Eskimo Nell, The Rocky Horror Picture Show, Applause* and *The Tempest*, and remains busy in the theatre, recently appearing in *School for Scandal* and in the musical *Guys and Dolls*, playing Nathan Detroit. In addition to all that, he's a regular in pantos, many of which he directs.

Christopher will always remember his time on *Porridge*. 'The most memorable episode was "Men without Women", with Fletcher drafting a letter for his fellow prisoners. When the audience suddenly realised the character called Trevor was Lukewarm's boyfriend, there was an almighty roar. It was probably the biggest laugh I've ever heard in a studio.'

McLaren

Scottish-born McLaren was brought up in an orphanage and since the age of fourteen has been in and out of care homes and prison. His early years were spent in Greenock, where a policeman had found him abandoned in an alley, protected from the elements by nothing more than a copy of the *Glasgow Herald*. He never knew his father and was unwanted by his mother, so no one was surprised when he drifted into crime. An aggressive, outspoken prisoner with a chip the size of Ben Nevis on his shoulder, he's serving a three-year sentence. McLaren works as a hospital orderly.

Tony Osoba was playing a manservant in *Churchill's People* when the offer to play McLaren came along. The character first appeared in 'Ways and Means', the penultimate episode in series one, and at the time Tony believed the role was a one-off. 'It was a great part because the character featured quite strongly. In the episode, McLaren, who was always hot-headed, winds up on the roof. Fletch comes up with one of his schemes and manages to talk McLaren down, but it was all engineered so that they both come out smelling of roses! I enjoyed the role but, at that point, there was no talk of the character becoming a regular.'

That was remedied when a second series was commissioned and McLaren became a fixture of the show. Tony was impressed with Clement and La Frenais' scripts. 'Most people probably thought that a comedy in prison was a most unlikely setting – and it probably took all the skill those guys possessed to make it succeed. I don't think too many people could have pulled it off; but their writing was so brilliant they ended up making the audience feel sympathetic towards the prisoners, even though they were being punished for their own wrongdoing. The sympathy was directed towards the inmates, not poor old Mackay and Barrowclough.'

The experience of recording episodes of *Porridge* was a happy one, as Tony recalls. 'The actors were given leeway to develop their characters, which is always pleasing, and the scripts were beautifully written: I can't remember any other show I've done where the scripts were tinkered with less. The atmosphere was such that actors were allowed to voice their opinion. Dick and Ian were often around for the read-throughs, but they never sat there as if they were protecting their precious baby – they were always prepared to listen to what others had to say.'

Tony particularly enjoyed working alongside Ronnie Barker, someone he regards as 'very generous'. 'He was the leading man, but if he saw moments where another character was doing something and it was funny, he would be the first to suggest dropping some of his own lines in order to incorporate it; obviously he was comfortable in his own abilities.'

Tony doesn't feel there was a weak episode in the entire series. 'There were some very funny episodes, then others which touched on people's feelings and sensitivities; Dick and Ian were able to couple these elements together without being maudlin or over-sentimental. I was delighted to be involved in the series, and always remember the utter disappointment if a script arrived and I wasn't in it. It's a bit of a cliché but I did get up and look forward to the day ahead because it was a joy being part of the programme.'

Tony also found the experience educational, learning a great deal about his craft from those around him. 'To be with actors of Ronnie, Richard, Fulton and Brian's calibre was wonderful. If you had anything about you, you couldn't help but observe and learn from these people – it was a superb schooling. I also owe a huge debt to Syd Lotterby. He would always encourage you and never make you feel small; if you had an idea, for example, which didn't work out, he'd never scoff.'

When the series came to an end in 1977, Tony – who went on to appear in the first episode of *Going Straight* – was very disappointed. 'It was a sad day, knowing we weren't doing any more, because it was a joy to work on. Everyone was given their fair share of lines and scenes; maybe there was an episode in which you didn't feature much, but then you'd get several nice scenes in the next. The rehearsals were good fun, and you found yourself going to work with a spring in your step, knowing you'd have a good day.'

If Glasgow-born Tony had pursued his childhood ambitions, he'd be employed as a car designer. 'By the time I was ten I could name every car on the road; I loved everything about them and would happily have lived and eaten my meals in a car. When I was thinking about going to university, I wrote to the car manufacturers to find out the best degree to study but soon discovered that no one could guarantee I'd ever be employed as a designer. I naïvely thought I'd be taken on as a designer and be creating these wonderful cars in just a few years. So I finished my A levels and made a sudden decision to become an actor.'

Tony trained at the Royal Scottish Academy of Music and Drama, during which time he was offered small parts in theatre and television. Upon graduating, he joined a Richmond-based theatre company, touring schools, before moving on to mainstream theatre, including spells working abroad and with the Royal Shakespeare Company.

Alongside his developing stage career, Tony was being cast for various television roles, with his first substantial feature part being Lawrence in *Churchill's People*. Among his 200-plus television credits are three series as Detective Constable Jarvis in *Dempsey and Makepeace*, parts in *The Professionals, Brookside, Bergerac, Minder, Doctor Who*, the role of Peter Ingram in *Coronation Street*, Barrett in *The Bureaucracy of Love* and Detective Superintendent Garrett in *The Bill*. Though he has continued to work in the theatre, including a couple of years spent with the Young Vic and various theatrical assignments in the States, since the eighties most of his work has been on the small screen.

Navy Rum

The loud-mouthed Navy Rum is one of the prisoners selected to help dig drainage ditches for the local council. Plastered in tattoos and with his long hair and beard, he cuts a rather daunting figure. Before turning to crime, he worked as a stoker on the tankers sailing the Persian Gulf. While he's been behind bars, he's served time at various prisons, including a spell with Fletcher at Maidstone.

Paul Angelis, who played Navy Rum, was offered the role after bumping into Ian La Frenais outside a London Tube station. 'We got talking and he told me he was filming *Porridge*. He asked if I'd be keen to play a character whom he described as looking like the bearded sailor on Players' cigarette packets.'

Paul accepted and headed for the location filming near Merthyr Tydfil, sporting a stick-on beard. 'It didn't stop raining, which meant we had to be careful because I had tattoos drawn all over me and they would have probably run if they'd got wet!'

Paul enjoyed playing Navy Rum so much he wished the character had developed into a regular. 'It was one of the most enjoyable jobs of my career, and it was lovely to watch Ronnie Barker at work.' But, alas, Navy Rum wasn't seen again.

Paul is a Liverpudlian who left school and began a career in merchant banking. He remained in the industry six years before auditioning for the Royal Scottish Academy of Music and Drama. After winning a full scholarship he joined the Academy in 1963, graduating two years later. He moved to London and earned his Equity card touring with a children's theatre company. A couple of fringe productions followed before Paul broke into television and went on to make early appearances in a number of shows. These included *Z Cars* (he was seen in 150 episodes as P.C. Bannerman), *Theatre 625*, *Callan*, *The Sweeney*, *The Liver Birds* (as Polly James' boyfriend), *George and Mildred*, *Robin's Nest*, *Juliet Bravo*, *Bergerac* and *Honey Lane*. More recent TV credits include: *Boon*, *Casualty* and *The Bill*, ten episodes of *Coronation Street* as Alf Roberts' chauffeur, a policeman in *EastEnders* and Reg Titley in the 1999 series *The Grimleys*.

On the big screen, he provided voices for the Beatles' movie *Yellow Submarine* and appeared in *Otley*, *Battle of Britain* and 1981's *For Your Eyes Only*.

Paul has also written for more than thirty years, including a food programme for TSW and several shows for BBC radio. He's currently working on a novel.

Norris

'Nasty' Norris makes his only appearance in 'Happy Release', sharing the prison's infirmary with Blanco and Fletch while having his in-growing toenail removed prior to his release. When Fletch discovers the obnoxious Norris has diddled the aged Blanco out of all of his worldly goods, he ensures

Norris gets his comeuppance when he leaves Slade Prison.
Fletcher devises a plan and tricks Norris into digging up a
football pitch (which in reality was Loftus Road, home of
Queen's Park Rangers) in search of some loot. His actions
result in him being arrested again.

Actor Colin Farrell feels he has lots to thank Norris for,
because playing the part helped him to overcome his dislike for
recording comedy in front of a live audience. 'I hadn't done a
lot of work with a live audience before *Porridge*, partly
because I hated it.' Colin regarded it as an 'awful medium' and
after some early experiences vowed never to do it again.

'Then I met Sydney Lotterby and was offered Nasty
Norris.' Although he held reservations about the type of
work, he couldn't resist playing the character. 'I'm glad I
accepted the part, because I learned so much from it such as
how to stay within the context of the scene, as well as not
thinking about the audience unless you were considering their
response to a potentially funny line. It's no good ploughing
on with the dialogue if the audience are laughing at an
earlier line; you have to wait for the laughter to subside.'

Prior to his taking up acting, for London-born Colin it
had looked as though a musical career beckoned: he was
playing instruments at seven, and belonged to the London
School Symphony Orchestra by eleven. But by the time he
started national service in the army, Colin's attention had
already veered towards acting. He'd studied for several terms
at RADA, and completed his course after giving up his
uniform.

After beginning his professional career in weekly rep at
Worthing, he got a lucky break by joining the original cast of
Chips with Everything at the Royal Court in 1962, later
transferring to the West End. Colin worked in theatre five
years before making his television debut in a production for
the BBC's *The Wednesday Play*.

Throughout the sixties and seventies, he remained busy on
the small screen, appearing in shows like *Dixon of Dock
Green*, *Armchair Theatre*, *Play for Today*, *Softly Softly* and

No Hiding Place. In recent years, he was seen in six series of *In Loving Memory*, and in *Heartbeat, The Bill* and *Midsomer Murders*. On the big screen, meanwhile, his career has included pictures such as *Oh! What a Lovely War, Gandhi* and *A Bridge Too Far*, playing Corporal Hancock.

Nowadays, Colin spends most time in the theatre; such work has included a spell with the Royal Shakespeare Company and six years touring the world with the English Shakespeare Company.

Rawley

Stephen Rawley, who's married to Marjorie, is sentenced to three years after being indicted for bribery and corruption. He is a friend of the Governor's: they served in the Guards together at Winchester, belong to the same club and socialise frequently. It's rumoured that their amity is the reason Rawley is given a cosy job in Central Records – something that irks Fletcher, whose anger is fuelled by that fact that his new cellmate was the judge who sentenced him.

Rawley arrives on the scene in 'Poetic Justice' and by the end of the following episode, 'Rough Justice', sees his appeal accepted. Rawley's weakness had been a younger woman: a nineteen-year-old go-go dancer he met at his regimental reunion when she was assisting the magician. When she became increasingly demanding, his troubles began.

Veteran actor Maurice Denham was called in to play the disgraced judge, just one of hundreds of roles he's performed on stage, screen and radio during his extensive career. Born in 1909, Maurice made his name as sundry comic characters in the 1940s radio shows *ITMA* and *Much-Binding-in-the-Marsh* before kicking off his busy film career with *Home and School, Daybreak, Fame is the Spur* and *The Man Within*. Other credits include: *Dear Murderer, London Belongs to Me, Landfall, Don't Ever Leave Me, No Highway, Street Corner, Carrington VC, Doctor at Sea, Sink the Bismarck!, Two-Way Stretch, The Heroes of Telemark* and *Danger Route*.

Scrounger

Scrounger helps make up the party given a day out digging drainage ditches on the moors. His knowledge of such tasks – he worked for a road gang on the motorways – may be the reason he's selected for the job. While touring the country's roadways before reverting to crime, he lived in a caravan with his wife and two children.

Johnny Wade was cast as Scrounger in the episode 'A Day Out', but it wasn't the first time he'd worked alongside Ronnie Barker, having already appeared in *The Two Ronnies* and the sixties show *Frost Over England*. Although he associates the part of Scrounger with several wet days filming in Wales, he enjoyed the experience nonetheless. 'It was good fun. The writing was superb and the characterisations perfect, especially Mackay,' says Johnny. 'I think Fulton had every drill-sergeant down to a tee, what with the sarcasm and the chin stuck out! The show had a lot going for it, particularly the rapport between Barker and Beckinsale.'

Born in Bethnal Green, Johnny started his working life as a singer after winning several talent contests. His days were spent running a market stall, selling sweets, while in the evenings he was busy working initially in cabaret and then with a band. Then he earned his television break, as a singer in the sixties soap-drama *Compact*, and played Stan Millet for three years before moving on to hit musicals, including *Guys and Dolls* and *South Pacific*, touring the world for more than three years. He's also worked at the Royal Court.

Johnny has remained busy on the box, appearing in *Z Cars*, *Coronation Street* (playing a lorry driver), *United* and four series as Roger in Yorkshire TV's *You're Only Young Twice*. Recent work has seen him appear in *EastEnders* as a drunken chauffeur, as well as in the second series of *Sunburn*, filmed in Portugal.

Spider

The creeping Spider looks after Grouty by fetching, carrying and running errands for him. He's seen in 'A Storm in a Teacup'.

Spider was played by John Moore, whose television work includes appearances in *The Avengers*, in 1961, as Ted Watson in a 1980 episode of *Juliet Bravo*, and as Joe in *Bergerac* a year later. On the big screen, he was seen in several films, such as *Countess Dracula* (1971), *The Frozen Dead, Captain Nemo and the Underwater City* and *Tess*, in 1979.

Spraggon

Spraggon, who was seen in 'A Test of Character', longs to be a writer, though his bad grammar, inability to spell and penchant for brutal language leave a lot to be desired. His cousin Ernie was a notorious tearaway and Spraggon longs to gain as much publicity as he did. Nicknamed Spraggs, his manuscripts are checked by Barrowclough in the episode while the education officer is unavailable.

Alun Armstrong, who played Spraggon, was born in Annfield Plain in 1946. He's worked on stage and screen, with his television appearances including *Whatever Happened to the Likely Lads?, The Stars Look Down, Sharing Time, This Is David Lander, Breaking Rank, Inspector Morse, Goodbye Cruel World* (as Gerald Faulkner), Uncle Teddy in *The Life and Times of Henry Pratt* and Austin Donohue in *Our Friends in the North*.

His film credits include: *A Bridge Too Far, Get Carter, The Fourteen, The French Lieutenant's Woman, White Roses, Split Second* and *Patriot Games*.

Tolly

Tolly, who's married to Norma, is one of the prisoners in 'Men without Women' who takes Fletcher's advice and sends his wife a letter – drafted by Fletch.

Tolly was played by actor Emlyn Price, who has also appeared in television shows such as *Bergerac, Remington Steele, The Bill, Boon, The Cabbage Patch, Rock Follies* (as Derek Huggin), *By the Sword Divided* (playing Corporal Veazey), *Roll Over Beethoven* and, more recently, as a policeman in 1995's *Cynthia Payne's House of Cyn* and as Neil Copeland in *Surgical Spirit*.

Tulip

Tulip appeared briefly in 'The Desperate Hours' as a fellow inmate given the disputable privilege of sampling Fletch's wine in the prison toilet. We learn nothing more about the character during the series.

Michael Redfern's appearance as Tulip in an episode of *Porridge* was just one of a myriad of shows he's appeared in. Born in Isleworth, Middlesex, early television work included Rufus Pargeter in *The Newcomers*, appearances in *George and Mildred*, as a policeman in *Robin's Nest*, and in *The Professionals* and *Agony*. Other small-screen credits include: *Never the Twain, United!, Hi-De-Hi!, The Gentle Touch, Minder, Terry and June, Sorry!, The 19th Hole*, Mr Cooper in *Bottom, The Bill, The Detectives* and *Hope and Glory*.

Reg Urwin

Reg Urwin, who'd worked for some time in the machine shop, replaces Keegan as the trusty tasked with serving the Governor his daily cup of tea. An unstable character, Urwin

has been recommended three times for psychiatric treatment in the last two years. He even tried committing suicide once: intending to steal a tin of luncheon meat in a supermarket, he suddenly wondered what his world had come to. Depressed with his lot in society, he put his head down and charged towards the glass doors.

Urwin takes advantage of his new lofty position and takes Barrowclough hostage in the Governor's office, demanding ten grand and a helicopter. It's down to Fletcher to save the day.

Dudley Sutton, who played Reg Urwin, boasts a lengthy list of credits, particularly on both small and big screen. On television, he's worked on numerous productions, including *The Avengers, Department S, The Baron, The Saint, Dempsey and Makepeace, Boon, Bergerac, Armchair Theatre, Shine on Harvey Moon, The Beiderbecke Affair* (as Mr Carter), *Lovejoy*, playing Tinker, and as a tramp in *Emmerdale Farm*.

Meanwhile, his film work has included *Go to Blazes, Rotten to the Core, One More Time, Diamonds on Wheels*, McClaren in *The Pink Panther Strikes Again, The Big Sleep, George and Mildred* (playing Jacko), *Chain Reaction* and *Orlando*, as King James I.

Warren

Bunny Warren is dyslexic and relies upon fellow inmates to read his letters from home, including those from his wife, Elaine, who lives in Bolton and was responsible for coining his nickname, Bunny. Prior to life behind bars, Bunny worked in his father-in-law's ironmongery in Bolton. Although not the brightest of guys, he's always high-spirited, a rare thing at Slade.

When we first meet Warren, he's served ten months of his sentence, and blames dyslexia for his plight: he claims he had a tough break – he couldn't read the sign saying 'Burglar Alarm' and got caught!

Playing the doltish Bunny Warren was Mancunian actor Sam Kelly. Turning his hand to such a dull-witted character posed no problems. 'Syd Lotterby had used me before in an episode of *The Liver Birds* in a similar role, so when the part of Warren, a rather simple-minded chap from Bolton, came up he asked me to play that as well.'

Sam didn't need anyone to tell him how to play Warren; it was evident from the writing. 'The scripts were brilliant and just reading them brought the characters alive; there's been hardly anything that's reached the level of those scripts since.'

But in retrospect he admits he'd have played the character differently. 'I hadn't done an enormous amount of television at that time. Now I would have made my performance more subtle and less broad as a piece of acting.'

Sam enjoyed his days at Slade Prison and rates it among the highlights of his comedy career. 'It was clear from day one that the scripts were second to none, and in Ronnie I was working with a genius – I learned a lot from him. He was extremely generous: he knew he was the star of the show and consequently could afford to be generous towards other actors to make the show better.'

A few years later, Sam worked with Barker again, this time in *The Two Ronnies* stage show touring the country, including a spell at the Palladium and Down Under. 'My main function was to play Bunny Warren in a scene specially written for the show. It was only twenty minutes long but I enjoyed it.'

It doesn't surprise Sam that the sitcom continues to attract large audiences whenever it's repeated. 'It was based on characters rather than jokes and worked well; but its setting is also timeless; and until they demolish Victorian prisons they'll be able to carry on showing it, which is very nice for my bank manager,' he says, smiling.

Born in 1943, Sam trained at LAMDA after working for three years in the civil service in Liverpool. He graduated from drama school in 1967 and was soon spotted uttering one line as a newspaper reporter in an episode of *Emergency – Ward 10*.

Four years of rep work around the UK followed, including spells at Liverpool, Sheffield and Lincoln. 'I became an actor because I wanted to work in the theatre, and for me television work subsidises the theatre work. Then every now and again you get a little gem on TV which makes you realise what fun it can be.'

On the small screen, Sam's credits include a series of *The Dave Allen Show, The Dick Emery Show*, playing Bob Challis in *Coronation Street*, Mr Snagsby in *Bleak House*, Norman in two series of *Now and Then*, Dr Geering in three series of *'Allo, 'Allo*, Grunge in two series of *Haggard* and Sam in three series of *On the Up*.

Sam, who's also appeared in a handful of films, including two *Carry On*s and the *Porridge* movie, remains a busy actor: he's recently completed a ten-part series of Carlton's sitcom *Barbara*, and there's another television project on the horizon as well as his annual stint in panto.

Blanco

Sixty-three-year-old Blanco Webb is a bespectacled old-timer who served seventeen years before receiving a pardon, in 'Happy Release', for a crime he insisted he didn't commit. Back in 1959, he was found guilty of killing his wife and hiding her body in a fridge, although he always stated her lover was responsible. He shared a cell with Lukewarm at Slade Prison and was a cheating Monopoly player. And Godber described him as being kind and gentle – but that was before he'd discovered that Blanco murdered his wife's lover.

Blanco has no family and leaves his friends behind at Slade for a life of loneliness. Reflecting on a past that saw him turn to stealing when he couldn't find employment, he's spent over half his life doing porridge.

Blanco was played by David Jason, regarded as one of the country's finest comedy actors. Forever busy on screen, David's glittering career has included such classic parts as the over-aged delivery boy Granville in four series of Roy Clarke's

Open All Hours, Pop Larkin in three series of *The Darling Buds of May* and Detective Inspector Jack Frost in *A Touch of Frost*. Considered by many to be his best performance, however, was the role of Del Trotter, the cheery wheeler-dealer in the long-running sitcom *Only Fools and Horses*.

Born in London in 1940, the son of a fish porter at Billingsgate Fish Market, David gained his first taste of acting as a fourteen-year-old in a school play. When he left school the following year, though, he followed his parents' advice and took a trade. He was initially a garage mechanic and then, after a year, switched professions and began training as an electrician; his evenings, meanwhile, were occupied performing with local amateur productions.

By the mid-sixties, David had turned professional and followed his brother, Arthur, into the world of greasepaint and footlights. Appearing at Bromley Rep in a production of Noël Coward's *South Sea Bubble* was the start of an award-winning career spanning more than three decades.

David made his television debut in 1967's children's comedy *Do Not Adjust Your Set*, alongside Michael Palin, Eric Idle and Terry Jones. He combined stage and television work for years, with appearances in *Crossroads* and in *Hark at Barker*, with Ronnie Barker, with whom he'd work so successfully years later.

Williams

Williams is a dour Welshman whose general mien makes you wonder if he should be residing in a mental institution rather than Slade Prison. A bit of an oddball, he claims to possess a large sexual appetite – compensating, perhaps, for his years of deprivation at a choir school.

Philip Madoc, who was cast as Williams, was born in Merthyr Tydfil. After working as an interpreter in German, he entered the industry in the 1960s, studying at RADA. He worked for a while in rep before moving into TV, one of his first appearances being in the 1956 production *The Count of*

Monte Cristo. Other TV work includes: Detective Chief Superintendent Tate in *Target*, Fison in *A Very British Coup*, and roles in *The Avengers* and *Doctor Who*. He also appeared as Angel Martes in 'Get Me Out of Here!', an episode of *The Champions*, as Rawlins in a *Randall & Hopkirk (Deceased)* episode titled 'Never Trust a Ghost' in 1968, and an episode of *Man in a Suitcase*.

Philip has also made more than thirty films, including *The Quiller Memorandum, Daleks: Invasion Earth 2150AD* and *Operation Daybreak*, while recent years have been dominated by theatre work including many classical roles. His own TV detective series, *A Mind to Kill*, in which he plays the lead, has been sold all over the world.

The Unseen Lags

During the series, Fletcher and the others frequently referred to unseen inmates, such as SMUTTY GARLAND – a.k.a. Slade's king of porn – in E-wing and TOMMY MCCREADIE, who was planning an escape route back to the arms of his nervy wife, a raver who's being sleeping with a limbo dancer. In 'The Hustler' we also hear about NIFTY SMALL, who's in love with Gruesome Glenda – a female social worker who visits the prison on Tuesdays.

In 'A Night In', we learn that MIGHTY JOE BANKS was Godber's previous cellmate. Fletch describes him as a 'head-case' because he set light to his own and Godber's mattresses. He was also the ringleader during a riot (that saw him throw a screw off the top landing), which led to his transfer to another prison.

In Series Two, Ives talks to Fletcher about RONNIE ARKWRIGHT, who tried strangling his wife on visiting day when she told him it was her last visit because she was off to live with a Maltese 'ponce' in Morecambe. CORKSCREW CARTER, a former solicitor before opting for a career behind bars, is mentioned by Fletch in 'Happy Release'. The non-speaking SID, meanwhile, plays draughts with Fletch in the early scenes of 'The Harder They Fall', while we discover BILLY MOFFAT is a rival to Grouty because he's running an unauthorised book for the boxing match. Other unseen inmates linked to the boxing event are NESBITT, Godber's opponent in the match, BIG MAC, favourite for the heavyweight bout ever since he put four warders in hospital after his jigsaw was knocked over, and LARRY, who's Godber's silent sparring partner.

In 'No Peace for the Wicked', Warren wants to play table tennis with MINI COOPER but can't because they haven't got a ball, while LUGLESS DOUGLAS sends them off to Fletch to get one.

We hear about TOMMY SLOCOMBE's tunnel in 'No Way Out': while prisoners sing carols at full volume, Tommy digs frantically in his search for freedom. A despicable bloke, his brother-in-law is a London villain and a friend of Harry Grout. His father, meanwhile, is Billy 'the ponce' Slocombe who escaped from Brixton in 1972, ending up on a sun-drenched Caribbean island where he's now chief of police! Helping with his escape is INKY STEPHENS, the finest forger in the country, who prepared his passport. Before the episode is out, the doctor mentions DONALDSON – who's serving five years for grand larceny and embezzlement.

ARSENIC RIGGS, who's serving time for poisoning, comes from Newcastle-under-Lyme and Fletch discusses him with Mackay in 'Poetic Justice', while in 'Rough Justice', CHARLIE GILL, who's also known by Fletch, got caught trying to escape because, being deaf, he didn't hear the dog chasing him.

In 'Pardon Me', there's reason to celebrate when the popular Blanco is awarded parole. Other prisoners whose cases are heard at the same time are GIBSON, in for car theft, whose appeal is declined, and MAC BROWN, serving time for manslaughter, who's delighted to be heading home when his case is surprisingly accepted.

We hear that a prisoner called GOMEZ passed his Spanish O level the previous year in 'A Test of Character', while in the final episode, 'Final Stretch', with Godber once again out in the wide world, Fletch's new cellmate is a Sunderland lad called NICHOLSON.

THE STAFF OF SLADE PRISON

Mr Appleton

Mr Appleton, a prison officer who works in Slade's kitchen, is seen in 'The Hustler'.

The character was played by the late Graham Ashley, who was also seen in shows such as *Doctor Who*, back in 1963, *Doctor in the House* (as a policeman), and as D.S. Tommy Hughes in the long-running police series *Dixon of Dock Green*. He appeared in various films, including *Track the Man Down, Man Accused, The Tell-Tale Heart, The Fast Kill, Alfie Darling, Adventures of a Taxi Driver* and 1977's *Star Wars*.

Chief Prison Officer Barrett

Chief Prison Officer Barrett made his sole appearance in a scene during 'A Day Out'. When Mr Mackay fears the worst and thinks the working party has gone missing, he apprises the Chief of the grave situation. It's clear that Mackay reports to the character, although we never hear from him again.

The Chief was played by Arnold Peters. Born in London in 1925, Arnold – who's the voice behind Jack Woolley in the long-running radio series *The Archers* – joined a dance band as a schoolboy until being called up to the RAF during the Second World War. Upon returning to civvy street, he became a professional actor and entertainer, with his first job being on radio's Children's Hour, in a programme called *Hastings of Bengal*.

Offers of work were plentiful and he joined the BBC Repertory Company in Birmingham. As well as radio and theatre work, Arnold is also a busy screen actor. His television appearances include: *Citizen Smith, Please, Sir!, The Siege of Golden Hill, Shoulder to Shoulder, United!, The Tomorrow People* and, in 1998, the BBC series, *Prince Among Men.*

Arnold has had a long-standing interest in English folk music and plays in a folk dance band.

Mr Bayliss

Mr Bayliss is Slade Prison's PT instructor and is seen in 'The Harder They Fall', training the prisoners for the forthcoming boxing tournament.

Bayliss was played by Roy Sampson, whose other credits include playing a policeman in *The Sweeney*, Harry Johnstone in an episode of *Doctor Finlay's Casebook*, Dougie Allen in 1991's *Advocates I* and the foreman of the jury in the 1992 film *Under Suspicion*.

Mr Birchwood

Mr Birchwood works as a prison officer at Slade and was seen in 'Just Desserts'.

John Rudling was a Londoner who qualified as a draughtsman before making his mark as a dependable character actor, beginning with the RSC. He moved on to work at the Players' Theatre, London, before touring with ENSA.

Repertory work as both actor and director kept him busy until film and television work came his way. His occasional big-screen appearances included the Ealing comedies *The Ladykillers, The Man in the White Suit* and *The Titfield Thunderbolt.*

On TV he's best remembered as Brabinger, the aged butler in *To the Manor Born*, but during the sitcom's run he suffered a heart attack. John died in 1983 from respiratory complications.

Mr Collinson

Mr Collinson was first seen in 'A Night In' as the prison officer who enters Fletch and Godber's cell. A sour-faced individual, Collinson is certainly not the life and soul of the officers' Christmas party.

Paul McDowell had already worked with Ronnie Barker on *The Two Ronnies* and *The Frost Report* before donning the prison officer's uniform in *Porridge*. Paul was given the freedom to develop his character's style. 'Mr Collinson was a very repressed sort of guy, someone who didn't get much out of life. He had a very sour outlook on humanity in general,' says Paul, smiling. 'He's probably married and miserable because of it, and if he'd had children, which was unlikely, they wouldn't have turned out very well.'

A successful writer himself, Paul can recognise when he's handed a decent script, and there was no doubting the quality of Clement and La Frenais' work. 'The writing was superb,' he says. 'It was a beautiful job, not a spare line, and it holds up so well even today. And the combination of Ronnie and Richard was just magic.'

Paul, who was born in London, left school and trained to be a painter at Chelsea Art College. During his student days, he formed a band, The Temperance Seven, and went on to enjoy success with six hit singles, including 'You're Driving Me Crazy', which went to number one in 1961. When Paul tired of the band, he left and worked at The Establishment, a satirical club in London, as a writer/actor, which introduced him to the world of acting.

Upon leaving the club, he worked in the United States for five years with an improvisational group, The Second City, before returning to England and writing for *The Frost Report*. His first small-screen appearance as an actor was in the second series of *The World of Beachcomber*, with Spike Milligan. On the box, he's worked predominantly in comedy, including many series with Dave Allen, *The Good Life, Only Fools and Horses* and four series of LWT's sitcom *The Two of Us*, playing Nicholas Lyndhurst's father, Colin Phillips. He was frequently cast as a policeman.

He's also made several films, including, in the role of a Scottish laird, *The Thirty-nine Steps*, with Robert Powell, and as a postman, 1980's *Rough Cut*.

Nowadays, Paul spends most of his time writing or teaching t'ai chi around the world; he's also had a novel published and hopes it will shortly be adapted for the screen.

Mrs Heskith

Mrs Heskith, the Governor's secretary, is seen in 'Disturbing the Peace'.

Madge Hindle was born in Blackburn in 1938 and spent her early years in amateur theatre. The role of Mrs Heskith was just one of many appearances she's made on the box. She made her debut in *On the Margin*, a drama series written by Alan Bennett, but it was her appearance as Lily in *Nearest and Dearest* that made her a household name. She went on to appear in sitcoms such as *Open All Hours* and *The Cuckoo Waltz* before spending four years behind the counter of the corner shop as Renee Bradshaw in *Coronation Street*.

Her more recent work has included playing Mrs Chadwick in *The Bright Side*, Mrs Shurer in *Lost Empires*, Elaine Dodswell in *The Rector's Wife*, and she appeared in *Anorak of Fire* and as Doreen in the 1999 series *Barbara*.

Dorothy Jamieson

Dorothy Jamieson takes over as the Governor's secretary from Mrs Heskith, and is seen in 'The Desperate Hours'. During the episode we discover she's been having an affair with Mr Barrowclough, although he tries dismissing the matter by claiming it's only a peccadillo.

Mrs Jamieson was played by Jane Wenham, who has made several film appearances, including roles in the 1950s' productions *The Teckman Mystery, An Inspector Calls* and *Make Me An Offer*. Her small-screen roles include those of Luciana in *The Comedy of Errors*, Portia in *The Spread of the Eagle*, Mrs Brittain in *The Testament of Youth*, Dolly Partridge in *Nanny* and Sophie in *Anastasia: The Mystery of Anna*.

Medical Officer

Slade Prison's Medical Officer wasn't in the best of health when he made his only appearance in 'New Faces, Old Hands'. Coughing and spluttering, he's tasked with inspecting the three new arrivals: Heslop, Godber and Fletcher. By the time we get to 'Happy Release' it's a different incumbent examining Fletch.

John Bennett, who played the spluttering medical officer in 'New Faces, Old Hands', has appeared in a host of productions during his career. His more recent credits include Idas in *Jason and the Argonauts*, the stranger in *Mulberry*, and the Corcyran Representative in *The War That Never Ends*. He's also been seen in several recent films, such as *Bridge of Dragons, The Fifth Element, Last Fair Deal* and *Priest*.

Other TV credits include *Jonathan Creek, Heartbeat, Cadfael, Hunter, Bergerac, The Professionals, Blake's 7, Survivors, The Avengers* and *Danger Man*.

Tottenham-born Terence Soall played the medical officer in 'Happy Release'. Upon leaving school, a career in acting was not what he pursued – he decided to become a journalist, and worked in Fleet Street for an international news service.

Whilst serving with the RAF in Gibraltar in 1942, he joined a theatre group and played his first role as a rejected lover. He enjoyed his experiences so much that upon returning to home shores in 1946 he gave himself five weeks to find a job in the theatre, else he'd return to the world of print. Good fortune was on his side, and the West Riding Theatre Company offered him employment.

After six months with the company he found himself touring Italy and Austria entertaining the troops. Shortly following his return to the UK, he had made his West End debut and appeared on TV. His small-screen appearances include *Coronation Street*, *Z Cars*, *Stand Up, Nigel Barton*, *The Master*, *Anna Karenina* and *Oliver Twist*. He's also appeared in several films.

Terence's busy career has covered all strands of the profession, including fourteen years directing at a drama school in Birmingham, but he'll always have a soft spot for his one-off role in *Porridge*. 'It was an enchanting show,' he enthuses. 'The two leading actors were wonderful; in fact, Richard Beckinsale was one of the most charming men you could ever meet.

'When I arrived for rehearsals, this young man [Richard] came bounding up to me and said: "You're Terence Soall, aren't you? I've seen a lot of your work." He was a lovely man.'

Doctor

The Prison Doctor is proud of his infirmary's low admission figures, and won't allow anyone into his ward unless they're literally dying on their feet.

Graham Crowden played the doc at Slade Prison, just one of many characters he's brought to life during an extensive career. In the fifties and sixties he was seen on TV in shows like *Destination Downing Street* and *Harpers West One*. He went on to work on numerous other programmes, including *Star Maidens*, *Raffles*, *The Guardians*, *Callan*, *The Adventures of Don Quick*, *Fraud Squad* and *Danger Man*. More recent work has seen him appear in *Don Quixote* and *The 10th Kingdom*, both in 2000.

Prison Officer

We never get to know the name of the Prison Officer who opens the prison gates to let Barrowclough and Fletcher in

during 'The Hustler', but he was played by actor John Quarmby, who received £50 for the day's filming.

John, who's now seventy-three and has been acting for more than fifty years, was born in Liverpool. After two years' national service in the RAF, he joined RADA in 1949. Repertory work dominated the first twenty years of his career, although he began appearing on TV from 1956.

His small-screen credits include: *Callan, Doomwatch, Van der Valk, 1990, Fawlty Towers* (as Mr Carnegie in 'Basil the Rat'), *Juliet Bravo, The Comic Strip Presents, The Scarlet Pimpernel, The Invisible Man, The Importance of Being Earnest, Vanity Fair, Great Expectations* and, in 1999, the mini series *Oliver Twist*.

He's also appeared in several movies, such as *Black Beauty* and *Restoration*.

Vicar

When the Prison Vicar comes calling on Fletcher during 'No Peace for the Wicked', he doesn't realise he's just one of a number of people who've disrupted Fletch's plans for a quiet afternoon. The vicar pays the price when Fletch throws him over the balcony, an act that earns him three days in isolation, something Fletch regards as bliss!

Playing the vicar was Solihull-born Tony Aitken, who started acting at his boarding school in Hereford. After training as an English and drama teacher at St Mary's University College, he taught around the Richmond area while looking for acting jobs.

His first appointment came at Hornchurch Rep, followed by two seasons at the Bristol Old Vic, by which time he'd also started being offered small parts on TV. Early small-screen appearances include *New Scotland Yard, Z Cars* and *Upstairs, Downstairs*.

Tony settled in London and while he continued working on the stage, he became more active in television comedy shows. His credits include *Agony, Married Love*, several series of *End of Part One* during the seventies, *The Lenny Henry Show*, *Blackadder II*, *Hot Metal*, *Open All Hours* and *No. 73* in the eighties, and more recently, *Barbara*, *They Never Slept*, *Sharpe's Justice*, *Keeping Up Appearances*, *The Bill*, *EastEnders* and *Doctors*.

As well as acting, Tony also runs his own voiceover recording studio.

Geoffrey Venables

Geoffrey Venables, who's married to Muriel, is the prison's weak-kneed Governor who seems more interested in the well-being of his tropical fish than the running of the prison. His passion for the natural world sees him serving on the local committee of the RSPCA, as well as opening a prison farm. He's a negative-thinking character with an ingrained resistance to fresh attitudes and ideas, especially if they're put forward by prisoners.

The Governor was played by the late Michael Barrington, who'd known Ronnie Barker for years and appeared in *The Two Ronnies* on occasions. His widow, Barbara, knows her husband enjoyed playing the Governor. 'You've got to enjoy comedy, otherwise you can't do it. He tried watching the episodes whenever possible, but was a very busy man: he did a lot of plays in the West End and went to Broadway for a while.'

As well as leading a busy theatrical life, including an eighteen-month spell at the National Theatre in *Coriolanus*, Michael, who also made the occasional film, appeared in plenty of TV shows – usually in cameo roles. His credits include *Private Schulz* for BBC2 in 1981, but he made his debut in an early episode of *Maigret*.

Michael was born in Shropshire in 1924 and, after his parents died when he was sixteen, he had to fend for himself. He wanted to train as a vet but the war disrupted his plans; after working at a munitions factory for a while he joined the Royal Engineers and served in Egypt and Greece. When he was finally demobbed he decided to try his luck as an actor and attended the Birmingham School of Drama. After graduating he entered the repertory circuit and appeared at venues such as Coventry, Birmingham and Nottingham, before making his London debut at the Vaudeville Theatre in *Salad Days*, playing three roles. Stage roles were sandwiched between television and film parts, including the 1971 picture *Follow Me*.

'For the last twelve years of his life, Michael continued to act like mad despite being an ill man,' admits Barbara. 'It was a terrible wasting disease of the lungs and he needed a lung transplant, but it was too late.' Michael died in 1988 aged sixty-four.

Mr Wainwright

Mr Wainwright, whose nickname was Napper, is an unpopular prison officer seen in 'Disturbing the Peace'. His time at Slade is short-lived because his belligerent manner causes uproar in the prison, so he's swiftly moved on to pastures new. Fletcher knows Wainwright from his days at Brixton, so when he arrives to cover for Mackay, who's attending a course, Fletch is far from pleased.

Wainwright was played by the late Peter Jeffrey, who was born in Bristol in 1929 and educated at Harrow and Pembroke College before graduating from RADA. He worked in repertory theatres up and down the country – including a season at Bristol's Old Vic – before becoming a familiar face on the small screen. His TV credits included playing Philip II of Spain in BBC's 1971 classic *Elizabeth R*, Mr Peabody in *Jewel in the Crown*, Colonel Bernwood in *Lipstick on Your Collar*, *The Planemakers*, *Triangle*, *Rising Damp*, *Lovejoy*, *The Detectives* and *One by One*.

His notable stage work included being a member of the Royal Shakespeare Company for more than thirty years, while on the big screen he was seen in several pictures, such as *Becket* (1964), *The Odessa File* (1974), *Midnight Express* (1978) and *Britannia Hospital* (1982). Peter died in 2000.

The Unseen Staff

One of the first unseen members of the prison's staff we hear about in the scripts is GRUESOME GLENDA, whose name pops up in 'The Hustler'. She's the female social worker who visits on Tuesdays. Well-known for her bicycle and brogues, we don't need to see her to realise what she's like because Fletch sums her up nicely, commenting: 'You'd be hard-pushed having an erotic fantasy about her.'

A member of staff mentioned several times but never seen was MR GILLESPIE, the welfare officer. His name is first uttered in 'Ways and Means', when we learn he recently graduated from university. Prior to joining Slade Prison, he worked at Welwyn Garden City; and he becomes a little distressed in his new place of work when prisoners head for the worldly-wise Fletcher for advice instead of him.

In 'Just Desserts', Mr Barrowclough mentions a prison officer called MR MALONE, who discovered Fletcher's missing tin of pineapple chunks during a routine security check at the prison. He's never heard of again.

Fletcher talks about a MR PRINGLE in 'Heartbreak Hotel' because he slipped on some orange peel, fell down the stairs and consequently suffers from a bad back. And, later, in 'A Test of Character', Fletch mentions MR KINGSLEY, Slade's education officer.

WHAT THE AUDIENCE THOUGHT

One method the BBC employed to monitor public opinion of its shows was to conduct audience surveys after selected episodes. Such reports were completed for several episodes of *Porridge*, and make interesting reading. Those who took part in the survey became known as members of the BBC viewing panel and, after watching all or part of the selected episodes, expressed their views about the show via a questionnaire.

What follows are extracts from the research reports:

The Harder They Fall

'This had been a consistently funny show that did credit to all concerned, the star and supporting cast being often praised among many warm comments; indeed, several thought it situation comedy . . . in "a rare top class".'

'A small number wondered "if it is correct to laugh about prison life", especially if portrayed as too soft, and, when sometimes "too crude", there was also some feeling that the series did "social good" by making "pertinent points" about certain problems and "increasing understanding" of prison life.'

The Desperate Hours

'Although felt by a few to be less than vintage *Porridge*, depending more on situation than verbal humour and tending to drag a bit at times, the programme clearly delighted most of those reporting and raised hopes for the return of a series widely held to be one of the best-written and most amusing in recent years.'

'The dialogue was excellent, some of Fletcher's almost throw-away lines being quite brilliant, viewers felt, and the situations well thought-out; two or three commented particularly on the assurance with which the plot changed direction from its light-hearted opening to the hostage sequence – still funny, but with an underlying seriousness.'

'While there was little scope as regards setting, etc., the production was usually commended, those reporting finding the prison background very convincing.'

Poetic Justice

'Whilst some disliked the confrontation between Fletcher and the judge who committed him, considering the situation "contrived" and the resulting conversations "too philosophical" to be really amusing, the large majority thoroughly approved of this "unconventional" plot, some particularly welcoming the opportunities it offered for an inclusion of a more "reflective and serious" element in the comedy.' 'Widely recognised as extremely well written, this was felt by most viewers to be another "hilarious programme" in one of the best and most intelligent comedies on television, very few actually disliking it to any degree.'

'The response to Ronnie Barker's portrayal of Fletcher was overwhelmingly appreciative. For many his "natural and outstanding" talent as a comedian "made the programme", and it was felt to be a measure of his ability that all the complexity of Fletcher's character was conveyed in such a manner that it served to make him at once credible and hilarious. Richard Beckinsale . . . was thought by most to be an excellent foil for Ronnie Barker, but was also praised in his own right.'

'Apart from a few criticisms that the pace and settings "lacked variation", the production was considered professional and "faultless" by most viewers.
    Creating . . . an "almost frighteningly genuine" and authentic prison atmosphere, the setting, costumes, etc. were all applauded. Overall, a smooth-flowing and realistic production of an excellently performed and written comedy.'

Final Stretch

'The sample expressed themselves delighted with yet another witty, funny and extremely entertaining episode in which humour and sentiment were skilfully blended and which provided an excellent finale to the series.'

'Viewers were also loud in their praise for the performance of, among others, Fulton Mackay, Brian Wilde and, particularly, Richard Beckinsale . . . As one wrote: "Although it is Fletcher's Cockney wit which gives the show its appeal, undoubtedly the other actors who portray the warders, the Governor and the other prisoners made it a punishment *not* to watch *Porridge*."'

Audience Figures

PILOT (First shown on BBC2) **PRISONER AND ESCORT** 1.4 million

PORRIDGE

(All episodes shown on BBC1)

SERIES ONE

1 **NEW FACES, OLD HANDS** 16.1 million

2 **THE HUSTLER** 13.8 million

3 **A NIGHT IN** 13 million

4 **A DAY OUT** 15.2 million

5 **WAYS AND MEANS** 15 million

6 **MEN WITHOUT WOMEN** 12.1 million

SERIES TWO

1 **JUST DESSERTS** 14.3 million

2 **HEARTBREAK HOTEL** 14.4 million

3 **DISTURBING THE PEACE** 16.2 million

4 **HAPPY RELEASE** 16.2 million

5 **THE HARDER THEY FALL** 16.4 million

6 **NO PEACE FOR THE WICKED** 16.8 million

SERIES THREE

1 **A STORM IN A TEACUP** 15.4 million

2 **POETIC JUSTICE** 15.6 million

3 **ROUGH JUSTICE** 15.7 million

4 **PARDON ME** 15.4 million

5 **A TEST OF CHARACTER** 15.2 million

6 **FINAL STRETCH** 15.7 million

CHRISTMAS SPECIALS

NO WAY OUT 18.5 million

THE DESPERATE HOURS 20.8 million

GOING STRAIGHT (All episodes shown on BBC1)

1 **GOING HOME** 13.8 million

2 **GOING TO BE ALRIGHT** 14.8 million

3 **GOING SOUR** 12.6 million

4 **GOING TO WORK** 14.1 million

5. **GOING, GOING, GONE** 15.6 million

6 **GOING OFF THE RAILS** 13.3 million

PORRIDGE – THE FILM
(FILMED IN 1979-80)

First broadcast on British Television: **Friday 31 December 1982**
BBC1, 9.15 p.m.

<u>CAST</u>

Norman Fletcher	**Ronnie Barker**
Lennie Godber	**Richard Beckinsale**
Mr Mackay	**Fulton Mackay**
Mr Barrowclough	**Brian Wilde**
Grouty	**Peter Vaughan**
Bainbridge	**Julian Holloway**
The Governor	**Geoffrey Bayldon**
Beal	**Christopher Godwin**
Oakes	**Barrie Rutter**
Rudge	**Daniel Peacock**
Warren	**Sam Kelly**
Ives	**Ken Jones**
Banyard	**Philip Locke**
Dines	**Gorden Kaye**
McMillan	**Oliver Smith**
Armstrong	**Andrew Dunford**
Wellings	**Steven Steen**
Simkin	**Ivan Steward**
Small	**Derek James**
Urquhart	**Karl Howman**
Callaghan	**Rod Culbertson**
Lotterby	**Zoot Money**
Cooper	**Derek Deadman**
Atkinson	**Robert Putt**
Whalley	**Allan Warren**
Whittakar	**Stewart Harwood**
McLaren	**Tony Osoba**
Hedley	**John Barrett**
Morgan	**Paul Barber**
Hayward	**Sebastian Abineri**
Samson	**John Dair**
Delilah	**Barry James**
Jacko	**Jackie Pallo Jnr.**
Tinkler	**Robert Lee**
Cox	**Robert Hamilton**
Miller	**Charles Pemberton**
Lassiter	**Colin Rix**
Collinson	**Paul McDowell**
Medical Officer	**Michael O'Hagan**
Chalky	**Paul Luty**
Weatherman	**Duncan Preston**
Alf	**Bunny May**
Sheila	**Elizabeth Knight**
PC Townsend	**Nicholas McArdle**
Old Lady	**Jean Campbell Dallas**
Old Man	**Bill Kerry**

Production Team

Screenplay by . . . . **Dick Clement and Ian La Frenais**
Producers . . . . **Allan McKeown and Ian La Frenais**
Director . . . . **Dick Clement**
Production Manager . . . . **David Wimbury**
Second Unit Director . . . . **Ian La Frenais**
Assistant Directors . . . . **Richard Hoult and Peter Kohn**
Director of Photography . . . . **Bob Huke, BSC**
Camera Operator . . . . **Freddie Cooper**
Follow Focus . . . . **Peter Biddle**
Script Supervisor . . . . **Jane Buck**
Editor . . . . **Alan Jones**
Art Director . . . . **Tim Gleeson**
Music Supervisor . . . . **Terry Oates**
(Song 'Free Inside' written by Lem Lubin and Ian La Frenais, sung by Joe Brown)
Wardrobe Master . . . . **Daryl Bristow**
Make-up . . . . **Sarah Monzani**
Hairdresser . . . . **Wendy O'Halloran**
Sound Editor . . . . **Jim Roddan**
Sound Recordist . . . . **Clive Winter**
Boom Operator . . . . **Ken Weston**
Dubbing Editor . . . . **Jim Roddan**
Dubbing Mixer . . . . **Paul Carr**
First Assistant Editor . . . . **Dina Eaton**
Technical Adviser . . . . **George Flanagan**
Production Assistant . . . . **Lindsay Sterne**
Casting . . . . **Esta Charkham**
Production Accountant . . . . **Mike Smith**
Assistants to the Producers . . . . **Georgie Dyer and Robert Vehon**
Props Buyer . . . . **Jill Quertier**
Construction Manager . . . . **Tony Graysmark**
Property Master . . . . **Jack Towns**
Craft Services . . . . **Sylvie Weston**
Stills . . . . **Albert Clarke**
Publicity . . . . **Sue D'Arcy**
Processing by . . . . **Rank Film Laboratories Ltd**
Filmed with . . . . **Panavision Equipment**
Lights by . . . . **Lee Electric (Lighting) Ltd**
Costumes supplied by . . . . **Bermans and Nathans Ltd**
Titles by . . . . **GSE Ltd**.

Certificate: . . . . **A**
Distributor: . . . . **ITC**
Production Company: **Black Lion Films (A Witzend Production)**
Length: . . . . **8,425 feet, 93 minutes duration**

Read All About It!

The movie's release received plenty of attention from the British media, but, in line with most of the examples within this genre, the conversion from small to big screen didn't impress the majority of critics, as the following reviews reveal.

'The plot is undernourished . . . and the good lines few and far between'

> John Coleman, *New Statesman*, 27 July 1979

'The plot is no more substantial than might sustain one TV episode (but it's 90 minutes instead of 30)'

> Valerie Jenkins, *Evening Standard*, 19 July 1979

'There is a lot of merriment to be savoured yet the film never loses sight of the grim realities of prison life that lurk beneath.'

> Ian Christie, *Daily Express*, 21 July 1979

'The Dick Clement and Ian La Frenais TV series makes a happy transference to the big screen, with a fair number of predictable prison jokes, an authentic setting . . . and a truly hilarious football-match climax.'

> Margaret Hintman, *Daily Mail*, 20 July 1979

'*Porridge* suffers . . . from the total lack of ambition that generally afflicts British television spin-offs . . . But, considering it was accomplished in less than a month and with a strictly limited budget, Dick Clement's film is very professional.'

> Derek Malcolm, *Guardian*, 19 July 1979

THE FILM

Fletcher and Godber are already doing porridge when three new faces arrive at Slade Prison: Beale, an arrogant warder, Rudge, a sullen first offender serving two years, and Oakes, an incorrigible long-termer who's halfway through a twelve-year stretch for armed robbery.

Fletch attempts to show Rudge the ropes and demonstrate how, with a little effort, he can adjust to life inside. Oakes, meanwhile, knows the score only too well and soon teams up with Harry Grout, the prison's self-appointed Godfather; after he promises to swell his bank account with a fat, juicy lump sum, Grouty agrees to orchestrate his escape.

To help execute the plan, the unfortunate Fletcher is dragged into the affair. He's tasked with persuading the prison officials to organise a football match against a showbiz eleven, a way to divert the warders' attention. While the match is in progress, Oakes will escape via the visiting team's coach.

The plot goes virtually to plan and Oakes is soon heading north; the trouble is that he ends up taking Fletch and

Godber with him. Keen not to tarnish their records, they leave Oakes and try sneaking back into Slade Prison underground, resurfacing through a manhole cover in the storeroom behind the Prison Officers' Club.

The 1970s saw a vogue for making movies out of successful television sitcoms. From *On the Buses* and *Bless This House to Are You Being Served?* and *Man About the House*, hardly a show was spared. Sadly, most offerings were flimsy versions of the small-screen originals, lacking the pace and intensity that made their respective shows successful in the first place. Most of the film plots left a lot to be desired, resembling over-stretched episodes, agonisingly spread over ninety minutes. But there were exceptions and – though many of the reviewers in the British press didn't appear to think so – *Porridge*, written by the Dick Clement and Ian La Frenais partnership, stood out from the crowd.

Dick acknowledges the challenge involved in writing sitcom-based films, and indeed has his own reservations about this one. 'You've got to pace it differently and ensure you have a story that sustains the greater length of screen time. I liked the film, but its weakness was that we didn't quite get the big laugh I wanted at the end – when Fletch and Godber returned to prison. The biggest laugh is the sequence where the new screw's bicycle is stolen but that's in the middle of the film – it's a shame. In hindsight, the scene should have been a bigger sequence, towards the end of the film.'

By the time the idea to make a film of *Porridge* arose, Dick and Ian had already formed a production company with Allan McKeown, whom they'd known for years and who, alongside La Frenais, went on to produce the picture. 'We all started working together in the early 1970s and, just before I moved to America, in 1976, we started a company, initially making television commericials,' says Allan.

At the company's inception, one of the first decisions the threesome faced was what to call it – never an easy task, and it was Dick Clement's then wife, Jenny, who inadvertently solved the problem, as Allan explains. 'We couldn't think of anything until Jenny stared at the three of us, looking rather bemused, and said: "What a hapless group you are, you look like you're at your wits' end." We suddenly thought, "What a great name for a company."' So the company was christened Witzend Productions; and when Dick and Ian moved to the States in the mid-1970s, they set up office in California.

It was when plans for an American series fell through that the time seemed right to consider making a film of *Porridge*. Allan – who's married to actress Tracey Ullman – had the job of securing a deal for the big-screen adaptation. 'I always told Dick and Ian that if they decided to make a movie of the show, I felt confident I could get the project financed.'

When a deal couldn't be struck with Columbia, Allan met executives at ITC, among them Lew Grade. The British film company snapped up the chance to transfer Clement and La Frenais' runaway success to the big screen, and assigned the project to its low-cost production wing, Black Lion Films. One of the things Allan admired about Lew Grade was his decisiveness. 'He'd listen to your pitch, then make a decision – there was none of this. "I'll get back to you next week". He was the greatest guy.'

Grade delighted Allan with his decision, then announced the size of the budget. 'He said: "The only thing is, you've

got to make it for £250,000." I agreed and we discussed the deal: we were to be fifty-fifty partners. But a couple of weeks later, Lew phoned and said: "We'll have to amend the deal because I can't let you be partners as far as television is concerned; there's no problem on the cinema side but I've got to keep television to myself." I agreed but with hindsight that was probably a mistake, because the film has been repeated on TV endlessly. However, I was green in those days and it taught me a lesson.' Allan nonetheless has no real regrets and enjoyed making the film.

Dick Clement, meanwhile, relished the chance of directing the picture. 'Everyone we spoke to, including Ronnie Barker, was interested, so we sat down here in California and wrote a script very quickly, then cut it down to size.'

As with its small-screen forerunner, locations would play a vital part in the film, and thus Allan couldn't believe his luck when a friend mentioned that Chelmsford Prison was temporarily empty. Other than the occasional scene – such as the escape sequence, which was shot in Buckinghamshire, and a glimpse of prison gates at Maidstone – the entire film was set in prison, so the chance of filming in a *real* jail was too good to ignore. Allan sought permission. 'There had been a fire inside one of the wings, so all the prisoners were moved out while the prison was refurbished. Fortunately parts of the prison remained intact and didn't need decorating; it was these areas I wanted to borrow.'

A meeting was convened with a Home Office official, and proceedings couldn't have started better when Allan discovered the head of the Prison Service was an ardent fan of the sitcom. 'The great thing about *Porridge* was that everywhere you went people had such incredibly strong feelings for the series and the characters. Luckily, we were granted permission, a lease was drawn up and, I think, I became the first person to lease out one of Britain's prisons.'

The agreement allowed the film crew to utilise the prison's hospital, workshop, a wing and the grounds; with the help of a production designer who built some interior sets, everything was soon in place. 'I visited other prisons with the designer and came away with ideas that we implemented. We didn't have a very good kitchen, so we built our own set.'

'We also built our own cell,' adds Dick Clement, 'which we used for pick-up shots. I filmed as much as possible in real cells, but when I needed to move walls around I used the constructed cell because it gave us more freedom.'

Once the final scene was in the can, it was time to pack up. This period of clearing up usually takes up to a week, but Allan remembers the mass exodus of crew desperate to leave the prison far behind. 'It can take days for everyone to clear up, especially for the electricians to remove all the wiring. After a month in prison they couldn't get out fast enough and the place was empty within a day! It was a grim location, and the weather had been very cold.'

Dick Clement concurs with Allan. 'It was a bitterly cold winter and a horrendous shoot because we had to film at weekends and fairly unsociable hours; I remember shooting for thirteen consecutive days. Whatever the budget of a movie, that's a savage schedule.'

With editing complete, the film was premièred in London before its distribution around the British Isles and abroad, including in the European and Commonwealth countries where the sitcom had become a hit. Allan McKeown was satisfied with how the film fared upon its release. 'Whenever you make a film based on a television series there is always a problem inasmuch as the TV series, by its very nature, is repetitive; you know it's on every week for half an hour and it's in little short bursts. Turning it into a ninety-minute film means there's a different dynamic, and it's fair to say that in the film there are parts where you expect it to finish and it doesn't – it goes on. Like in most movies, there's padding, but overall I think it worked well.'

Although Ronnie Barker agrees with Allan, he admits that the genre isn't his favourite medium. 'With films there's lots of stopping and starting which makes it disjointed: one minute you're working on an early scene, then you jump to another at the end of the film; it wasn't as enjoyable as the situation comedy, it suits a half-hour slot better.'

Fortunately, many of the lags imprisoned with Fletcher in Slade Prison during the sitcom's run were available for the film, and the appearance of familiar faces in supporting roles was important in its overall success. Tony Osoba once again played McLaren, but he was disappointed when the filming schedule was hit by inclement weather and he had to leave the production early, resulting in his character playing a reduced role to that originally intended. 'It was a bittersweet experience for me. I was contracted to the film for four weeks, after which I had to go off and play Hamish in the television series *Charles Endell Esquire*. Unfortunately, the weather was atrocious and filming kept being postponed. Part of the movie involved a football match, but day after day it was impossible to film because of snow. Dick Clement tried shooting a scene here and there, but we got further behind in the schedule and by the end of my contracted time I'd only shot a fraction of what I was supposed to do. Eventually, I had to leave and a lot of my intended lines were given to other characters.'

Appearing as Warren, as he had in the series, was Sam Kelly, who enjoyed the job but with hindsight doesn't feel that the concept worked as well on the big screen. 'To me, it seemed as if the production team felt they had to reintroduce all the characters – perhaps for potential foreign markets – and that took up too much time. But it was fun to do, even though it meant spending time at Chelmsford jail.'

Establishing among its audience an understanding of the film's plot and characters was a deliberate act, as Ian La Frenais explains. 'Being that we were now working in a different medium, we couldn't take it for granted that everyone knew the series; we had to cater for those people who'd never seen the show on television – that obviously took a little while.'

When Allan McKeown considers the question of whether he would have tackled anything differently, given the chance, he concedes that he wouldn't have agreed to the deal offered by Lew Grade. 'I'd have paid for the film myself, owned the negative, and gone on to make plenty of money out of it – but then, I didn't have a quarter of a million pounds. So, at the time, we were thankful to Lew for putting up the cash.'

THE REAL PORRIDGE

HM Prison Chelmsford

Back in 1979, Rannoch Daly was Assistant Governor at Chelmsford Prison when Dick Clement, Ian La Frenais, Ronnie Barker et al came to film the *Porridge* movie at his prison. It's a period he remembers clearly.

I'd been home from my work as an Assistant Governor at Chelmsford Prison for a couple of hours on the evening of 20 March 1978 when I heard a shriek from my wife in the living room in response to a television newsflash. The prison was on fire. I lived about three miles away in Great Baddow. I grasped the scale of the incident a few moments later when I tried to drive to the prison. The police had cordoned off the whole town of Chelmsford and I had to negotiate my way through their roadblocks. On arrival I found twenty fire appliances in attendance.

The prison staff had managed to rescue all 217 prisoners out of their cells and into workshops, the staff canteen and prison hospital. By working throughout the night, the fire service brought the blaze under control, the police organised secure transport and the prison staff escorted the prisoners to Wandsworth and Pentonville prisons in London. The last prisoner to depart had, in fact, been on home leave the previous week with his family. He'd returned to the prison, as instructed, by 1100 hrs on 21 March – and read accounts of the fire in the morning newspaper while travelling by train from London, courtesy of British Rail. He arrived back at Chelmsford Prison just in time to catch the last bus out. By midday he was headed back to London: to Wandsworth Prison, courtesy of the Metropolitan Police.

The staff settled down to what we thought would be an uneventful two years working in other prisons until Chelmsford was rebuilt. The Governor, Bill Guinan, moved to Prison Service HQ and I remained behind as 'Acting Governor' of an empty prison, the envy of many colleagues!

Towards the end of 1979, an enterprising film producer called Allan McKeown telephoned the Home Office with a request he thought was unlikely to elicit a positive response. His company was called Witzend Productions so a certain tongue-in-cheek approach was, perhaps, *de rigueur*. Nothing ventured, nothing gained; he asked the Home Office if they could provide him with an empty prison in which to film *Porridge*.

To his surprise, they sent him to Chelmsford, just up the A12 from his mother's house in Hainault. In December he arrived to meet us with the assistant producer, David Wimbury, and director, Dick Clement. They wore immaculate suits and talked big business. It was clear from their initial tour of the prison that they thought it was the right location, but it was clear also that they needed the endorsement of Dick Clement's writing partner, Ian La Frenais. He came along the following week.

A deal was struck with the Home Office full of indemnity clauses, security conditions, access regulations and all sorts of other technicalities that only David Wimbury understood. As soon as it was signed, the team returned to prepare for filming. The immaculate suits had gone. In their place were trainers, jeans, jumpers and leather jackets and a new phase of Witzend Productions.

As can be seen in the film, it was winter: January 1980. Filming lasted about six weeks. For the stars and crew there seemed to be some nervousness about meeting 'real' prison staff in a real prison. For the staff and their families there was the buzz that accompanies the making of a film and the prospect of autographs. For me, there was the fact that most prison staff wear uniforms that make their identity obvious but the Assistant Governor doesn't. There were usually dozens of film people around, occasionally hundreds. I decided that I would advertise my presence among them by wearing some distinctive cold-weather clothing: my Strathclyde University scarf and a woollen ski hat. I think I was also trying to demonstrate that I didn't fall into the script image of a prison governor. Having now learned a little more about the skills of scriptwriters, I think I may have been lucky not to end up as the punch line to one of their jokes.

On more than one occasion there was a 'meet the stars' session in the prison for staff and their families. Ronnie Barker, Fulton Mackay, Richard Beckinsale and the others were mobbed as they patiently signed autographs, shook hands, posed for photographs, joked, laughed and entertained.

I discovered later that for each of them this celebrity business was actually hard work. Ronnie Barker was not naturally ebullient and jocular. He was a rather serious man for whom being a comic actor was a craft and a profession. On one evening my wife and I joined Ronnie, Allan McKeown, Dick Clement and their partners for dinner at their hotel. They all showed a keen interest in prison life, which was very frustrating, as I wanted to talk about how they made films. Some of this interest was politeness towards their guest; some of it seemed to be the natural curiosity about a closed world that I have observed in most people; and some of it seemed to be a professional interest in the work that I was doing and they were portraying.

Ronnie Barker's conversation homed in on relationships between staff and prisoners and it seemed to me that he and Dick Clement were paying rather more attention to the answers than is often the case with dinner companions.

I learned during this film production that the script often changes during shooting and that the first task each day is to check for and learn any 'pink pages' – script amendments. I discovered this quite early in the filming, when Allan McKeown presented to me a souvenir copy of the screenplay signed by himself, Dick Clement and Ian La Frenais. I was sufficiently star-struck that I spent the evening going through every word. Ian asked next day, 'Have you read it?' I told him I had, so he was keen to know what I thought of it. Friends who know me well will not be surprised to discover that I started telling one of our best television writers about the three points where I thought the text could be improved. However, they will be very surprised indeed to learn that later in the day jokes were beginning to circulate in the team about the 'Governor's pink pages'. Ian had incorporated two of my suggestions in script amendments. I allow myself a small smile of satisfaction when I hear them spoken in the film; but I notice even more the third point, where he did not accept my advice and where, as a consequence, Godber speaks a slight inaccuracy in his account of Scottish football!

Having discovered the script I then discovered filming: watching Ronnie Barker and his colleagues work a scene through from start to finish. The scene was in a dressing room during the football match when Fletcher is bringing an 'injured' player off the field [Oakes – played by Barrie Rutter]. The 'injury' turns out to be the prelude to an escape in the visiting football team's bus [driven by Gorden Kaye]. All that was being filmed was a few seconds as Fletcher and Oakes moved from the door to the bench and said a few words – something about an 'early bath'.

The scene was played through several times and, although it had looked pretty rough the first few times, I soon realised that there was an intentional 'layering' process at work. The basics were approached first (the traverse across the room, co-ordinating the movement of the two actors) before the words in the script were added and the sequence was run through several more times. All this then had to be practised in some detail with the sound recorder checking his levels and the lighting and the cameraman getting his requirements in place. Only after this had been done several times was an attempt made at getting the whole sequence down on film – 'Lights, Camera, Action!'

At this point it became apparent how much the players, Barker in particular, had been holding in reserve. It came across as a very simple scene. However, the complexity of the presentation and the extent to which it had had to be built up, layer upon layer, had been completely obscured by the apparently natural manner of the finished product as it appeared on the screen; art from artifice.

The filming attracted the attention of the newspapers and the local radio and television journalists. The *Chelmsford Weekly News* was kept busy, and the *Observer* sent Robin Lustig. *Woman's Own* did a feature article. There were a few minutes on BBC Television's teatime news and magazine programme, *Nationwide*. They broadcast me saying that 'compared to a real prison, both Godber and Fletcher were too old. Fletcher was too smart to keep coming back to prison in his forties and Godber, at twenty-four, was well past the age of the first-timer: most prisoners were aged seventeen to twenty-six and first came to prison in their teens.'

Richard Beckinsale approached me the next day in a quiet moment between takes. He'd seen the *Nationwide* snippet. What I had said had struck him. This was a fact that he'd not come across before. He was about thirty and had a wife and daughter. By his age most prisoners were already played out. He was perturbed. However, he also told me an amusing anecdote against himself as a performer. He'd recently been starring in a comedy in a West End theatre. One scene required him to disappear behind a shop counter looking for something and, a few seconds later, to bang his head on the underside of the counter coming back up. He repeated this night after night, getting a bigger and bigger bruise on the back of his head, until he worked out that if he used a hidden piece of wood to bang under the counter he could get just as big a laugh with no bruise. The real joke was that he was doing this gag seven shows a week but the length of time it took him to work out that he could use the wood instead of his head was eight months.

Sadly, a few months later Richard died of a heart attack. There was an awards programme of some sort on television a few days after his death. Ronnie Barker was there. He was ashen and dumbstruck.

On a quiet night, when he had little filming the following day, I invited Fulton Mackay to dinner at home with my wife, Evelyn, and our daughter, Lhosa, as a break from the hotel. He accepted. Mr Mackay and Fulton

181

Mackay shared a name and an appearance but had little else in common. In contrast with his screen persona, Fulton's conversation was littered with cultured references to writers, poets and, particularly, painters. Almost everything he saw or spoke of was expressed in terms of a picture or an artist. Although Evelyn's parents live in Scotland, her mother, Margaret, is German. When we asked Fulton to autograph a card to her, he thought for a few moments and then proceeded to inscribe the card in German – complete with a quotation from Schiller.

His *coup de théatre* came in his conversation with Lhosa, then aged two years and three months. At that age she was quite unselfconscious and also full of the new world of words. Among her repertoire was her full name and address; our precaution should she ever seem lost. Fulton spoke with her at some length and seemed very impressed with this, getting her to repeat her name and address more than once and congratulating her on 'learning her lines'. The next day we discovered that Fulton had been learning his lines as well. He sent a large bunch of flowers to Evelyn, correctly addressed as he had memorised from Lhosa.

Fulton invited us to come and see him later in a play he was about to rehearse at the Donmar Warehouse, called 'The Hang of the Gaol'. He said he would meet us outside the theatre thirty minutes before the start of the performance. We were five minutes late, having been detained elsewhere by Allan McKeown, and Fulton was beginning to fret because we were eating into the time he'd put aside for 'getting into the character'.

The play was set in a prison that had been destroyed by fire. As I understood it from Fulton, the author had seen a newspaper reference to the fire at Chelmsford Prison and used that as the inspiration for the play. Fulton played the Inspector of Prisons who'd been sent to inquire. There were a number of suspects, a few twists and turns in the plot and, in the end, it turned out that the person who had started the fire was the Governor. However, from the Home Office point of view, it just would not do to have a governor burning down his own prison so the Inspector was told to pin it on someone else. Needless to say it didn't take Fulton too long to find a prisoner who was delighted to take the credit for the destruction of the gaol.

After filming at the prison there were some scenes to shoot in the studio and there was the editing to do in the cutting room. A few weeks later, Allan McKeown invited Evelyn and me to join the cast at a preview theatre in Soho to see the finished product. We entered a nearby pub for a pre-show drink and were greeted by Gorden Kaye, Julian Holloway – who'd played the celebrity football-team manager – and the musician Zoot Money. The minor character he played was a prisoner called Lotterby, which seemed to be a tribute to the TV series producer, Sydney Lotterby.

In the version of the film eventually released, the song sung over the opening sequences is by Joe Brown. In the version I saw that day in Soho it was Ian Dury singing 'Hit Me with Your Rhythm Stick'.

A singular distinction befell Senior Officer George Flanagan. George had been at Chelmsford for many years but he was not quite as fit as he had once been, and he had lost any initial enthusiasm for working away from home in other prisons. We gave him the job of day-to-day liaison with the film crew as their guide and mentor. As his reward the crew gave him his place in history with his appearance in the credits as a 'Technical Adviser'; the only member of Chelmsford prison staff with his name on the film. However, he's not the only one to appear in the film. Behind the closing credits we see an officer and a prison dog patrolling into the evening. They were not actors; they were real.

To say thank you and farewell to Chelmsford once the film was ready for release, Allan McKeown hired a local cinema to give a private preview for staff and their families.

A REFLECTION OF REAL LIFE?

The film revolves around an escape. A gun is smuggled into the prison by a bus driver. The bus belongs to a visiting 'celebrity' football team. A prisoner called Oakes then escapes in the bus using the gun to force Fletcher and Godber to accompany him. The whole escapade turns out to be a scam set up by genial 'Harry Grout', the Mr Big among the prisoners (played by Peter Vaughan – magnificent years later in *Our Friends Up North*). After some curious adventures Fletcher and Godber manage to smuggle themselves back into the prison in the same bus. There are numerous other story lines (e.g. the new officer – Christopher Godwin) and sub-plots (e.g. Mackay's teeth) but the escape is the central event. Oakes gets away. Mr Mackay is outwitted. The Governor is embarrassed. Fletcher is in the thick of it but remains unscathed. The prisoners have a good laugh, so do the audience.

Of course, in real life, a gun in a prison is not funny. The staff would be scared but so would the prisoners, with the possible exception of the one carrying the gun. How do the writers make it funny? Do real prison staff and real prisoners find it funny? Yes, they do.

The attitude of most prison staff and prisoners to most prison settings in films and television is that they are overly simplistic (e.g. *Escape from Alcatraz, Prisoner: Cell Block H*). The key fact about imprisonment for most viewers or members of the public is that they have no personal experience of imprisonment and draw their assumptions from their knowledge that prison necessarily involves loss of liberty. This is then assumed to be the overpowering single element in prison life, with the prisoners and the staff always wholeheartedly antagonistic towards each other. In any fictional portrait of imprisonment a riot or an escape is to be expected.

The key insight of *Porridge* is that, once a person has been imprisoned and has to make a life within that imprisonment, their whole range of human emotions, relations and imagination come into play. The same is true of the staff. They vary in their character. They have to find a *modus vivendi* with the prisoners. To varying degrees they bring their life outside the prison into work with them. Fletcher bestrides this world because he understands the need of each party for the other. He knows the extent to which the staff have to settle for something less than total mastery of the situation and the prisoners can find some space in which to exercise some choices of their own. The prisoners can have 'little victories' and the staff can accept 'little defeats'.

That doesn't mean that everything the viewer sees in episodes of *Porridge* is a literal representation of what happens in real prisons in Britain. Neither art nor theatre nor film work is like that. The best analogy I can think of is with a political cartoon. The drawings of the participants are not accurate; rather they simplify and exaggerate recognisable features so that the viewer sees instantly who is portrayed. The drawing will also convey elements of character or mood.

Because of this richness of understanding on the part of the writers, *Porridge* is itself able to enter into the cultural world of the prison. One can see *Porridge* on television in a prison with the prisoners watching the television and the staff supposedly watching the prisoners. But the staff will quite probably also be watching the television, and the prisoners – some of them – will be watching the staff. When they each catch the other's eye it will be impossible to tell whether they are smiling at Fletcher or at Mackay; or at their recognition of themselves in these roles in real life; or at their recognition of the other party or at the other party's recognition of them. Mostly they are smiling because they each know that the dynamics they are watching on television are a true reflection of the dynamics they are experiencing in their own life and work in the prison. The most reassuring thing they can discover is that their perception is shared with their opposite numbers.

Despite its artificiality, *Porridge* is at least as accurate a reflection of its world as are the best cartoons. Mackay,

Barrowclough and the Governor, Fletcher, Godber and the rest all ring true. Prison staff enjoy them. Prisoners enjoy them. Those who know nothing of prisons enjoy them. But, in addition, they learn much more about prisons through the characters in *Porridge* than they could learn from any other source.

Here's what real-life prison officers thought about *Porridge*.

Sixty-seven-year-old George Forder spent thirty-four years in the prison service before his retirement twelve years ago. His career included working at the notorious Manchester prison Strangeways and, for seven years, at Parkhurst. He believes the humour of *Porridge* was very realistic.

Humour played a big part in the daily life of a prison. Without it long-term inmates wouldn't survive the system, nor indeed would many of the staff. It lightened the load and made the days bearable for both prisoners and staff. The humour of *Porridge*, although manufactured, was very true to life. Fletcher-types existed: they were often serving long sentences and would go to just about any length to frustrate the system, or to get what they wanted. They soon knew the weak and strong points of staff; we also got to know them in the same manner.

We had to protect the weaker, less able types. I remember one prisoner who was constantly being set upon and bullied by others on the same landing. We decided the only way to deal with the situation was to relocate him. So he moved in with one of the more aggressive inmates, who'd been told that the only way to guarantee a favourable hearing at the parole board was to ensure this chap didn't come to harm – it worked perfectly.

'The characters in *Porridge*, although rather extreme, are very accurately drawn. I've known all these types during my service, including the Mackays and the Barrowcloughs – though much has changed since I retired.

As for all the privileges bestowed upon Grouty, the bigwig among the prisoners at Slade, George recollects a time at Parkhurst when long-term inmates were allowed to keep caged birds, usually budgies, in their cells.

One of the routines rigidly adhered to was the Chief Officer's rounds. He would walk round the wings in the evening, not speaking other than to tick someone off, and then return to his office. One Chief Officer had the nickname 'Curlyboots' because the toes of his boots curled upwards.

An orderly – an inmate who looked after the requirements of staff by making tea, running errands, etc. – had a budgie which was a superb talker. It would fly around the wing in the evening, chatting away. One phrase it had been taught was: 'Look out – here comes Curlyboots!' Staff tended to congregate in the tea room, which wasn't really allowed because they should have been patrolling the landings. When the tea room was full, the bird would sit outside and screech at the top of its voice: 'Look out – here comes Curlyboots!' The room cleared in seconds, with staff running in all directions.

George recalls another incident that could easily have been lifted from the pages of a *Porridge* script. Two prisoners had escaped by cutting a hole through barbed wire; while one headed for a nearby forest, the other was found sitting on the pitched roof of the building, merrily throwing slates.

The whole place was surrounded by staff as the Governor and Chief Officer arrived on the scene – not unlike Mr Mackay and Mr Venables, the Governor of Slade Prison in the sitcom. A ladder appeared and was erected to reach the guttering of the building. I must give the Governor his due because he was first up the ladder, although he came very close to getting a slate on his head!

'Come along now, John,' said the Governor as another slate whizzed by. 'This is no way to behave; come down and let's talk about your problem.'

At that moment, another voice was heard saying: 'I'll get him down for you, Governor.' It was a prisoner whose face had appeared at a cell window. The Governor agreed to let him try, and ordered the Chief Officer to get the prisoner. The Chief, who was already on the red side of pink because of the situation, turned brilliant red and came very close to bursting a blood vessel.

'Governor, we have enough problems here already without adding to them,' protested the Chief Officer. But the Governor would have none of it: if the prisoner felt he could talk his fellow inmate down, it was worth a try.

So out the prisoner came and, after scaling the ladder, it wasn't long before he was sat up on the roof as well, shouting: 'Now try and talk me down!' By now, steam was coming out of the Chief's ears. The idea of getting the fire engine out and hosing them off was suggested, and by this time any suggestion would have been acceptable.

Being a fire officer, I went off to get the engine with some helpers. It was nothing more than an engine on a trailer, which pressurised the water from the hydrant. It had never been used in anger and from test runs I found it to be such a noisy, shaky thing that I wondered how it all kept together. We arrived back at the scene to find more slates missing and another ladder placed against the other wall for whoever was to direct the jet of water from the hose. The engine started without difficulty and the shaking and rattling began. The hoses were attached and an officer scaled the ladder with the hose. All was ready, and 'Switch on!' came the request.

When the water came gushing out the hose, the two prisoners took shelter behind the tall air-vents on the roof, but it wasn't long before one of the prisoners had had enough and asked to be let down. The other inmate, meanwhile, stuck it out and a hole had to be cut in the roof from inside to allow an officer access and eventually get the prisoner down.

Overall, *Porridge* was very true to life in prisons prior to the Mountbatten Report. There were plenty of schemers, fixers and twisters like Fletcher. They involved themselves in all sorts of activities that formed the 'underworld' of prison life. Many of these activities, although quite harmless, were against the rules, but blind eyes were cast.

There were the Mackays, whose attempts to bring life back within the rules were often frustrated – but that didn't stop them trying.

Garry Morton has been a prison officer for eight years. His father has just retired from the profession after completing thirty-five years' service, and his brother works in the profession too. All are keen fans of the sitcom.

Prison officers love the programme, and it's the only show that has ever shown the industry in a good light, of sorts; it's certainly the nearest thing to the actual job.

Many programmes are made in support of the police, hospitals, fire brigade and ambulance service, and they're all shown as heroes of society. I've always felt that we're the forgotten public service – and if there's anything that makes a prison officer proud about the job he or she loves, it's every time *Porridge* is on TV.

Even today, new recruits look upon it as a symbol of everything that's good about the job; and, although it's out of date in many respects, it's still a good reference. In *Porridge* there's no scandal or deep-rooted bad feeling, which every other programme about prison seems to show with enthusiasm.

Of course, the hero for us is Mr Mackay: he's the person everyone wants to be in a comical kind of way. Anyone who makes a mistake or looks concerned about anything is referred to as Mr Barrowclough.

I can remember a few years ago, when I worked at Brixton – which Fletcher always goes on about – we hung a photo of Mr Mackay in our landing office. One of the officers faked a signature on it with the comment, 'To all my friends at Brixton – bang 'em up!' Everyone loved it, including the prisoners – a few of them wanted a copy to put in their cells.

For the next few months, whenever there was a picture of Mackay or Fletcher in a paper or magazine, no matter how small, it was quickly torn out and displayed in various cells.

PORRIDGE

Peter Hunt is fifty-one and has worked in the prison service for more than twenty-eight years. He remembers being told when he started his career that *Porridge* provided an accurate picture of life within prison.

When I joined, back in 1974, I spent eight weeks at a training school near Bristol. While there, my principal officer told us that *Porridge* was starting and that he'd had a preview of it: if anyone wanted to know what prison was like, it was best to watch it. Because – although it was a comedy and certain aspects were over-emphasised in order to lift the comedy – it was basically a true reflection of prison life at that time. He also told us that we'd see every type of character in *Porridge* during our service – and he was right.

For a while, I worked in borstals and was probably more of a disciplinarian at that point, but I found myself working with a chap who was an ex-priest and like Barrowclough in many ways. When we were on duty together it worked well, because I could tell the inmates to sit down and be quiet, but if anyone had a problem, my colleague would take them to one side and have a chat; we complemented each other.

You get people who write dramas about prisons and they take dramatic licence by putting everything in to the scripts that could possibly go wrong, including riots. But anyone who knows anything about prisons knows that riots rarely happen.

With *Porridge*, although you had to allow for the stretching of the characters and the incidents in order to create funny scenes, I could relate to what they were focusing on – often the mundane little incidents, which happen frequently. In the days the sitcom was written, the toilet paper issued to prisoners was old, stiff, shiny stuff, and they often tried pinching the softer stuff issued to staff. Exploring incidents such as that is why the programme was much more realistic than anything else written about the prison service.

Chris Muzzal is a health-care officer at a prison in Surrey who's worked in the service for nineteen years.

We all know an officer like Mackay and a prisoner like Fletcher, and the humour is spot-on. The respect – with the undertones of dislike and disgust – shown by Fletcher to the 'screws' could not be closer.

Some of the incidents I've experienced during my time in the job would have made ideal scenes in the show. When I was working in the youth custody system, I had to escort two inmates to court. They were cuffed together, but still decided to do a runner after stepping out of the van. Unfortunately, ten yards down the road they encountered a lamppost and ran either side of it, resulting in them meeting nose to nose the other side. When we had stopped laughing, they were treated for a broken nose and a lump on the forehead.

I also remember a time when an officer was escorting a vanload of staff and prisoners to another prison. In those days – pre-1981 – a prison van was affectionately known as a 'Pixie', a shortened form of the term 'prisoners in transit' or PITX.

On this occasion, for a laugh, when an officer stopped the van for a call of nature, the other officers drove off. The stranded officer, thinking the prisoners may have stolen the van and taken the officers hostage, flagged down a passing police car and excitedly began babbling about 'the pixie that just left without him'.

Only a phone call to the Governor from a police cell saved him from a short stay in a mental institution!

PORRIDGE GOES ABROAD

Often when a successful British television series is adapted for the American market, much of the richness and vitality is lost in translation. Style of humour differs between the cultures; and, far too often, rather than trying out the original version, television companies set out to remodel the show's fabric to suit the different audience. Or that's the intention. More usually than not, the finished product fails to deliver the goods, is a wan shadow of its predecessor and swiftly disappears into oblivion, never to be heard of again.

Dick Clement and Ian La Frenais have experienced their fair share of adaptations for the US market, with varying degrees of success. *Porridge* was just one of their shows to receive the treatment. Titled *On the Rocks*, the series was set in the fictional Alamesa Minimum Security Prison and screened on ABC, running to twenty-two episodes shown between 1975 and 1976. Most of the action took place in Hector Fuentes' cell, which he shared with his friend DeMott, the optimist Cleaver, and young offender Nicky Palik. Patrolling the prison was the tough disciplinarian Mr Gibson, America's answer to Mr Mackay. The show was recorded in front of a live audience and contained location scenes at a real Californian prison. And, during 1975, it was the subject of complaints when the National Association for Justice asked ABC to abandon the series, believing it portrayed prison-life as too comfortable.

Producing *On the Rocks* was John Rich, who first heard about Clement and La Frenais when Warner Brothers sent him a script based on their sitcom *Thick as Thieves*. He was asked to make a pilot for the US market. 'The script had been written by an American and was about three people living together, yet there was a terrible flaw in it, and I told Warner Brothers so. When they asked what I meant, I replied: "These people are not related in any way: where's the conflict?"'

John – who directed *The Dick Van Dyke Show* and produced and directed *All in the Family*, the hugely successful US version of *Till Death Us Do Part* – asked to see Clement and La Frenais' original script to check if an integral element had been excluded from the American version. 'As soon as I received it everything became clear: two of the characters were married – only a small detail that had been left out!' says John, laughing. Though he ultimately declined the offer to make the pilot, he liked Dick and Ian's style of writing and decided to find out more about their work. Via their London agents, he spoke to both of them; after seeing some copies of *Porridge* scripts, he confirmed he could make an American version. 'I knew there would be some doubters because at the time it would be cutting edge material over here. I eventually met Dick and Ian and was instantly charmed because they're very nice people; of course they were attracted to me because I said I'd give them something they weren't used to getting in England. When they asked what it was, I replied, "Money!"' says John, with a smile.

'As far as money for writers is concerned, there's no comparison between the British and American markets, and Dick and Ian had been working for a pittance in British television. There's a lot to be said for the medium in Britain: writers can generate what they like, even if it's just a one-off, while in America it's a different animal and you've got to be prepared to write the same show for years. But the compensation is the money.'

John agreed to make Clement and La Frenais equal partners in the American production and they set to work converting their successful British sitcom. 'I helped Americanise the scripts and, although we made a mistake with the casting and found no equal for the Cockney lag, we mounted a sensible production and were on for twenty-two weeks. We could have stayed on if we'd wanted, but after discussions, Dick, Ian and I knew it hadn't worked out like we'd originally intended.' Despite the programme being generally well received, none of the partners were pleased with the results. 'We did something unheard of in American television and turned down an offer to carry on for a second year,' explains John. 'The writing was wonderful, and most of the casting was successful, but we made a mistake with the lead part – even though the audience didn't necessarily share our views. Overall, we did the right thing to call it a day.'

Dick and Ian were disappointed. 'The plots translated quite well,' explains Ian. 'We really felt it could work, and saw it opening up all sorts of possibilities. But everyone was terrified it was going to be too gritty for the American market, and it ended up being a poor version of the original.

'We worked our socks off with the scripts, but the trouble was we never had a Ronnie Barker. During the course of the week, all the rewriting was making the scripts more suitable for a gang show, cushioning the actor who played the main role.'

'We were very naïve, really,' suggests Dick. 'We came over to America and were offered a deal to make a pilot, and then felt we'd go on to write the American version of *Porridge*. In hindsight, it was a naïve attitude to presume such a thing because most pilots don't get made; that we succeeded with this one was against all the odds.

'The only problem was that it wasn't very good. We stayed with it for a year, wrote twenty-three episodes, including two rewrites – and I must admit it felt like being in the trenches. It was much harder work than in Britain because we never really found an American actor who could play Fletch the way we wanted. It was amazing that we were kept on the air, and we attribute that to the tenacity of John Rich, the director.

'It just seemed as if all the subtlety and nuances of the British series had been lost; we just knew it wasn't any good. I remember being in the studio until one o'clock in the morning doing retakes. In the end, the show was made in the cutting room, which wasn't the way we'd worked before, so we weren't happy one little bit.'

Dick and Ian yearned for their home comforts. 'We longed for the simplicity of the Beeb, where you'd do the show and be in the bar by nine-thirty, before going home with the satisfaction of knowing you had another one in the can. It was so painless and this was such a tortuous process.'

John Rich has always enjoyed collaborating with Dick and Ian. 'They can do no wrong as far as I'm concerned,' he enthuses. 'They're prolific, clever and very witty; their lines are delightful because they understand comedy and how human beings act. When I'm looking for writers, I like people who aren't afraid to say something in literary English, creating a situation, comedy moment or a joke that's not necessarily understood by everybody: I call it a two per cent joke.

'If people don't understand something, it's harmless and goes straight by them. But for the small percentage of the audience who can appreciate the writing, it's rewarding. Dick and Ian reach this level and I like that. It sounds like snobbery, but I never want to write down for the masses; I'd rather have them come up to us. With *On the Rocks*, Dick, Ian and I decided that the characters would speak a patois not dissimilar to what we hear in *Porridge*; these petty felons would never speak it but the fact that they had elevated conversation made the show different.'

While he was planning the American version, John Rich had the chance to travel to London – and watched in awe as Messrs Barker and Beckinsale rehearsed an episode. 'They were magnificent and I drooled over their comic timing – I just wished we had such talent in our country!' says John. 'We have a lot of very good actors over here, obviously, but Ronnie and the rest of the cast were just wonderful; I was particularly impressed by the way they handled language with a kind of rapidity, an element I would have liked in my version.'

Despite Rich's fondness for the British version, he's certain it wouldn't have caught on with American viewers in its original form. 'The references would have been unclear to the mass audience we have, partly because of the different cultural backgrounds. There is also a difference in the style of prisons: we have very vicious prisons in America and I don't think it would work to have a show like *Porridge*, set in a more gentle form of establishment.'

On the Rocks was well received and made money for its writers, yet is rarely repeated in the States. 'It's been assigned to the hallowed halls of yesteryear,' says John Rich, smiling. 'Sometimes it's resurrected for cable channels, but here you've got to have a giant hit to earn a repeat showing. *On the Rocks* attracted a cult following but not enough to justify a repeat run. But I still have many happy memories of working with Dick and Ian.'

ON THE ROCKS

Original transmission: **Friday 11 September 1975**

Last episode shown: **17 May 1976**

All episodes were shown on Mondays, 8–8.30 p.m.

CAST

Hector Fuentes	**José Perez**
DeMott	**Hal Williams**
Cleaver	**Rick Hurst**
Nicky Palik	**Bobby Sandler**
Mr Gibson	**Mel Stewart**
Mr Sullivan	**Tom Poston**
Gabby	**Pat Cranshaw**
Baxter	**Jack Grimes**
Warden Wilbur Poindexter	**Logan Ramsey**

CASHING IN

As is the case with many successful sitcoms, *Porridge* merchandise was available to fans. In 1977, BBC Records and Tapes released two episodes on LP. The record was manufactured and distributed on the BBC's behalf by Pye and contained 'A Night In' and 'Heartbreak Hotel' (catalogue no: REB270; price: £2.99). The project was edited and co-ordinated by Sylvia Cartner, and Don Smith took the cover photos.

The theme tune for the sequel, *Going Straight*, was also released on record. With Ronnie Barker singing words penned by Clement and MacCaulay, the track hit the public domain in 1978, with EMI releasing it under catalogue number 2768.

Four novels based on *Porridge* and one on *Going Straight* have been published. The first, titled *Porridge*, was adapted from the TV series by Jonathan Marshall in 1975, and a year later BBC Books released *Another Stretch of Porridge*, adapted by Paul Victor. Paul Victor reworked more scripts in 1977 when the Beeb issued *A Further Stir of Porridge* (£3 in hardback, 70p in paperback). The final title from the BBC focusing on the sitcom was Paul Ableman's *Porridge: The Inside Story*, in 1979. The book based on *Going Straight* was adapted from the series by Paul Victor and published in 1978.

Fans of the sitcoms may be interested in tracking down 1979's *The Porridge Book of Rhyming Slang*, by Ronnie Barker (Pan Books, ISBN 0 3303 0993 5, copyright Witzend Productions). Two of Clement and La Frenais' scripts have also been published: 1983's *Television Comedy Scripts*, edited by Roy Blatchford (Longman, ISBN 0 5822 2071 8), contained the script for the *Porridge* episode 'Poetic Justice'; David Self's *Situation Comedy* (Hutchinson, ISBN 0 0914 2931 5) included the script for the *Going Straight* episode 'Going to be Alright'.

The Beeb has released a handful of videos. *A Night In* (Ref: BBCV4799) contained the episodes 'A Night In', 'The Harder They Fall' and 'A Storm in a Teacup'; *A Day Out* (Ref: BBCV5844) offered 'A Day Out', 'Ways and Means' and 'Disturbing the Peace'; and a third, *No Way Out* (Ref: BBCV6206), included 'No Way Out', 'Pardon Me' and 'A Test of Character'. More recently, the BBC marketed a four-video boxed set containing every episode of the sitcom. Issued in a presentation gift box, the set retails at £39.99.

There have been various releases of the movie on video, including that made by 4Front (Ref: 0842583); Carlton has also issued it on DVD.

GOING STRAIGHT

In March 1977, we waved goodbye to Norman Stanley Fletcher in the final episode of *Porridge*. When Fletcher is finally released from Slade Prison, he takes with him not only the nightmares of being locked up in a cell for the last few years but also a tatty bag containing his worldly possessions. Those being: a tartan penknife, one brown belt, an African shilling, a tin of corn plasters, billiard chalk, Tottenham Hotspur keyring holding two keys, a receipt from a shoe repairer's for soling and re-heeling his brown brogues, and a 1974 Ladbrokes' pocket diary. But this wasn't to be the last we'd see of the old rascal, because plans were afoot to follow his uncertain path back into society as he headed south to his Muswell Hill home.

BBC executives had invited Dick Clement and Ian La Frenais to lunch at Television Centre; the final episodes of *Porridge* had just been shown and discussions veered towards the future. 'It was a lengthy lunch and didn't finish until five, by which time a great deal of wine and brandy had been consumed,' recalls Dick. 'It was all very jolly, and in the middle of this we suddenly started talking about *Porridge*; someone asked if we'd thought about doing another series. We felt it would become repetitive if we did that, but said we were interested in seeing what happened when he got out. Everyone loved the idea and it was virtually commissioned there and then.'

The wheels were set in motion, and by February 1978 Ronnie Barker was back on the screen playing donkey-jacketed Fletcher in the first of six episodes of *Going Straight*. Joining him was his long-standing cellmate, Lennie Godber, played again by Richard Beckinsale, together with Patricia Brake as Fletch's daughter Ingrid and Nicholas Lyndhurst in an early screen outing as Fletch's dense-looking son, Raymond.

Patricia had made three appearances in *Porridge*, but the character came into her own during *Going Straight*, becoming a pivotal figure in the Fletcher household, as acknowledged by TV critics. Writing in the *Observer* in March 1978, Clive James felt Ingrid possessed a 'fluffy but compelling sexiness' and that Patricia played her 'with all the low-life zing that Cockney sparrers of stage and screen are traditionally supposed to display but never do.'

One character missing from the series was Fletcher's wife, Isobel, who left him after twenty-four years of marriage. Her absence was partly due to Ronnie Barker's wish to avoid too much domesticity within the storylines, as Dick Clement explains. 'He didn't want to suddenly get into a conventional domestic situation with wife and kids; he wanted to keep it more unique than that, which, I think, was right. That's why we wrote his wife out, leaving him no alternative but to fend for himself.'

Although the cast brought their characters alive adroitly, there was a mixed reaction to the screening of *Going Straight*: from some quarters there came the strong feeling that no sequel would ever recapture the magic and richness of its prison-based predecessor. Even though the series represented a logical progression, removing the *Porridge* characters from their familiar situation and placing them in a new environment was no easy feat; many other such attempts within the history of the small screen have ended in dismal failure. But advocates of these views hadn't accounted for the scriptwriters behind the sitcom: Dick Clement and Ian La Frenais were past masters in such affairs. They had revisited the lives of their Likely Lads, Terry Collier and Bob Ferris, and scored a huge hit with *Whatever Happened to the Likely Lads?* which many people regard as better than the original sixties series.

So a new chapter in the life of television's most popular jailbird spotlighted him trying to forge a new life against the elements of society. Says Ian La Frenais, 'For Fletcher it felt like he was walking on eggshells, especially as he was on probation. Again he was fighting the system; you had to feel his frustrations about the predicament he found himself in, and what he hadn't achieved in life. You missed all the other characters in prison, but the series wasn't any more difficult to write; in fact, it was just as enjoyable and we scripted a couple of really good episodes.'

It was clear that Clement and La Frenais' new sitcom would be hard-pushed to ascend to the heights of its predecessor. Inside prison, Fletcher was a winner, whereas outside he wrestled with the harsh realities of a life he was unaccustomed to; he couldn't find a job, and struggled to get a foothold in an unfamiliar society. Fletcher, understandably, cut a forlorn figure outside, and some loyal *Porridge* fans didn't like the way their loveable felon had turned out.

In reviewing the success of the programme, opinions varied: those involved with the actual production didn't rate it as highly as *Porridge*. Sydney Lotterby, who produced both sitcoms, views it as a mere shadow of Clement and La Frenais' study of life behind bars. 'I thought it might have worked but the sadness is that it lacked the flavour of the original series. Also, the situation was nearer a normal situation comedy and the series suffered from a lack of clear identity.' However, he realises that it is tough to judge a show against a powerhouse sitcom like *Porridge*, and is disappointed that *Going Straight* rarely gets an outing into today's bustling TV schedules. 'I think it's as good as some of the programmes going out at the moment. The first episode in particular was excellent, with Fletcher and Mackay meeting on a train.'

Fletcher struggles with life outside Slade Prison

It's fair to say that some fans of the original series felt slightly pained by Fletch's struggle to adjust to the big wide world outside the relative comfort of Slade Prison. As a lag, he was familiar with a system and a pattern of life; he knew

how to eke out every ounce of goodness within an arid existence inside. His self-confidence, meanwhile, was boosted as
his experience of bird saw him adopt almost iconic status
within the prison, and he must have felt bucked by the
adoration received from so many of his fellow inmates, all of
whom held him in high esteem.

But once he left that world behind, and vowed never to
return, he found it difficult to turn his back on the life to
which he'd dedicated the lion's share of adulthood. Despite
the obvious harshness of his existence behind bars, and the
deprivations that go hand in hand with such, Fletcher
enjoyed there a sense of security and warmth – things he
struggled to find once he was out on his own. As he floun-
dered, his status suffered and he became a lost soul, unable
to claim a footing in his new environment.

Although Ronnie Barker agrees that the sequel didn't work
as well as *Porridge*, he enjoyed the experience nevertheless. 'It
wasn't as good, but there were some great people working on
it, and we had excellent stories, too.'

Inevitably, some viewers weren't convinced about the
show, either. The BBC organised an audience-research report
after the screening of the opening story, 'Going Home', and
discovered that a small minority echoed the views of other
critics. Some claimed to have 'found it harder to adjust to
Fletcher's new situation, feeling that the prison setting was
ideal and that *Porridge* had a special quality of its own,
which, they feared, would now be lost.'

However, much of the sample audience was more upbeat
about the show. The author of the report stated that the
opening story was 'warmly received by viewers', and that
'most people thought it an excellent idea that the series should
be extended beyond the confines of Slade Prison.' Such a
move could save the show from 'going stale and give it more
scope in the form of new situations and different locations.'

Overall, the sample audience who helped conduct the survey
were ardent fans of Fletcher; they were pleased to see him
back on our screens – one viewer went so far as to proclaim:
'I could not imagine television without Fletcher.' Others were

even quite happy to see him back inside, should circumstances dictate. The majority saw *Going Straight* as a 'logical progression' allowing Fletch the chance to set his wits against the outside world, and the fact he was able to 'transfer in this way made the series something out of the ordinary and special.'

The production and acting during 'Going Home' was regarded as top

Fans of *Porridge* had met Fletch's daughter Ingrid before, but she became a central figure in *Going Straight*

notch, just like that in *Porridge*, and more than ninety per cent of people expected to watch the remainder of the series. Although no episode attracted the ratings of the most popular instalment of *Porridge* ('Desperate Hours' was watched by 20.8 million), *Going Straight* never dropped below 12 million during its six-episode run.

Without doubt, *Going Straight* is an underestimated sitcom, forever overshadowed by its big brother, something reflected by the lack of repeats on mainstream television. There are plenty of inherent qualities in *Going Straight*, from the calibre of acting and production to the sleekness of the scripts, as highlighted by Clive James in his *Observer* review. He felt that 'no other country . . . can offer a television series like *Going Straight*.' He regarded the show as the worthy successor of

Porridge and thought every line written by Clement and La Frenais 'at least twice as good as anything in the average West End play.' James acknowledged Ronnie Barker's performance, but added that, 'The secret of successful comedy is so often looked for in the wrong place. The actor's personality matters, but last and least. First and foremost comes the work at the typewriter. It is because people have thought long and hard through many drafts that Norman Fletcher or Basil Fawlty can be convincing with a single gesture.'

Like the positive views shared by the majority of viewers, the media coverage on Clement and La Frenais' new sitcom was largely encouraging, though some journalists pointed out the difficult task facing the writers. Sean Day-Lewis, writing in the *Daily Telegraph* in February 1978, felt that Fletcher's creators were 'taking a risk in setting him free from the well-defined boundaries in which he previously flourished.' After watching the opening episode, Day-Lewis remarked that it 'showed how difficult it will be to match television's funniest situation comedy.' And, though he acknowledged the versatility of Barker at the helm, he felt that: 'the outrageous candour, cynicism and cunning, the spontaneous kindliness and charm of his Fletch began to diffuse a little even in the confined space of the train taking him home.'

With Fletcher out of prison, new locations were required. While Muswell Hill was picked for Fletcher's home, a hotel in Paddington was chosen for his place of work. Mike Crisp, the production manager, found both locations. 'I was pleased to find the hotel in Paddington, which was run by a sweet little man. I told him we were making a follow-on series to *Porridge*, with Ronnie Barker as a porter in a hotel. To help convince him, I reassured him that his property wouldn't be represented in any bad light and, in the script, the guy running it is very generous because he gives Fletcher a job. Basically, I was trying to persuade him to let us use the hotel, which, eventually, he agreed to do.

'If we were going to make out the hotel was a dreadful place we'd change the name, put up different signs, and you wouldn't be able to recognise it, but that wasn't the intention, so everything remained as it was. Later, I was tasked with writing up the publicity blurb and described the place along the lines of "Fletcher takes up a new career as a hotel porter in a modest hotel close to Paddington Station". Unfortunately someone altered the text and the episode was publicised with a synopsis that read something like: "In this week's episode, Fletcher gets a job in a flea-bitten, run-down . . ." As you can imagine, the owner wasn't very happy and it took a while to sort it out.'

Sydney Lotterby assembled a production team, most of whom had worked with him on *Porridge*. One new team member was make-up designer Christine Walmesley-Cotham, whose extensive list of credits includes productions such as *Vanity Fair* and *The Buccaneers*. She'd worked with Ronnie Barker on *The Two Ronnies*, and relished the chance of doing so again. 'He's one of our finest comedy actors, but hates doing a sketch or playing a character as himself – he always needs a tiny little moustache, sideburns, a pair of glasses, something to make him different. In *Going Straight*, of course, the character had red hair.'

The hair dye was applied before each day's filming, or prior to a spell in the studio. 'We used a spray, which worked well,' recalls Christine, who even remembers the formula. 'It was three squirts of red to one squirt of brown, before being plastered with loads of Brylcreem to make it shine.'

Christine, who now works freelance after more than two decades at the BBC, regards Ronnie Barker as a 'delight to work with'. 'His sense of timing was superb, as was his overall awareness of where he was at any given time in the production.' Although Ronnie agreed to take Fletcher beyond the prison cell at Slade, he'd already decided that, once the six episodes were complete, he would leave the character behind and return to *Open All Hours*. 'It was only ever going to be one series, because I didn't want to get stuck in the character – I wanted fresh challenges. But I liked doing it, and it was lovely working with Patricia Brake and Richard Beckinsale again. There were also other good actors, like Nigel Hawthorne and David Swift, and, of course, Nicholas Lyndhurst, playing my son.

'The first episode was excellent fun, because the story involved just Fulton and me on a train, with Mr Mackay getting more and more drunk. There's no doubt the series could have continued but the danger was it could have strayed further away from the original plot.'

In *Porridge*, the confinements of the prison cell induced an intensity unsurpassed by anything the sequel had to offer, but *Going Straight* was an interesting concept and deserved to be detached from its precursor and respected as a new entity.

Dick Clement feels *Going Straight* has been neglected over the years, but still regards it as one of his favorite pieces of work. 'Inevitably it was different and people say it wasn't as good as *Porridge*; maybe it wasn't – it didn't contain the same sort of security from being inside a contained environment. Nevertheless, it still had some funny moments, including the first episode where we also find Fulton leaving prison. But the final episode, "Going Off the Rails", is probably the best we ever did – I'm very fond of it. It's a good script and contains some nice textures.'

Dick is confident that were the series to be given an airing on mainstream television now, people would view it as a meritorious example of the sitcom genre. 'Some people were disappointed it wasn't *Porridge* and, of course, that had been the template, but *Going Straight* had lots going for it. Fletcher was very much a three-dimensional character, and Ronnie's performance as good as ever.' And just like with many of their previous pieces of work, Clement and La Frenais focused on the realities of life. 'He'd been inside a long time and faced real problems when he finally got out, so we tried confronting these predicaments. We've always done that in our scripts – otherwise you rely on a load of jokes, which doesn't appeal to us. People have been too harsh towards *Going Straight* and it will always be a favourite of mine.'

The Fletcher Family

Ingrid

Fletcher's eldest daughter is the bubbly, gum-chewing blonde Ingrid, whose confident, carefree attitude towards life saw her visit her father in prison without a bra. When a shocked Fletch broached the subject, she replied, 'I don't need to, Dad. I haven't done for ages – my breasts are firm and pliant.' There's certainly no doubting her popularity with the men.

Ingrid – whose middle name is Rita – is a qualified manicurist and, though her outspokenness and tarty appearance may not be to everyone's liking, she has a heart of gold and is a hard worker. When her mother leaves home, she runs the house at 107 Alexandra Park Crescent as well as holding down a full-time job before finally marrying Lennie Godber, who's been working as a lorry driver since his release from prison.

Actress Patricia Brake was presented with an unexpected award after playing Ingrid in the *Porridge* episode 'Heartbreak Hotel'. 'It's a certificate of bralessness!' says Patricia, smiling. 'The prop boys made it for me and I hang it in my bathroom; it reads "Patricia Brake appears braless" – which I did. Even though the episode seems tame compared to today's standards, it was quite risqué at the time because no one appeared on television without a bra.'

Patricia enjoyed playing Ingrid. 'In the first *Porridge* episode I appeared in I had very little to do, but I think I made the writers laugh – from there the character grew. The scripts were wonderful and it was great working with Ronnie Barker.'

Though Ingrid became a central character when *Going Straight* was written, and even though she appeared in only a handful of *Porridge* episodes, Patricia preferred the prison-based series. '*Going Straight* didn't work so well as *Porridge*, probably because the character had so much to fight against inside. But I enjoyed them both; there aren't many decent characters written for women, so I was jolly lucky being in something as good as those two shows. You're only as good as your scripts and fortunately Dick Clement and Ian La Frenais were brilliant writers. It was classic comic writing because as well as making you laugh the scripts could make you cry.'

When she started playing Ingrid, her father went along to watch the recording at Television Centre. 'Ingrid was very tarty-looking and my father didn't recognise me – I couldn't believe it!' exclaims Patricia, who was in her twenties when she played the role. 'I was young and earnest at that time; everything was so important and I know I felt in awe most of the time.'

Born in Bath, where her father was a butcher, Patricia always wanted to be an actress. Upon leaving school at sixteen, she joined Bristol's Old Vic Drama School. Immediately after completing her two-year training, she became assistant stage-manager at Salisbury Rep. Her duties included playing every juvenile part going. 'It was a wonderful grounding, because you played an assortment of roles – you learn such a lot that way.'

After Salisbury she appeared in a fifteen-minute television series, *Home Tonight*, before performing – aged just eighteen – at Stratford as Hermia in *A Midsummer Night's Dream*. The busy start to her career continued with more small-screen offers, including a part in *The Ugliest Girl in Town*, an American production filmed in the UK. After the exposure of appearances in *Porridge* and *Going Straight*, Patricia made guest appearances in numerous comedy shows, such as Eth in *The Glums*, *Seconds Out*, Di in *Singles*, Cherry in *Troubles and Strife* and Central's sketch show *Mike Reid's Mates and Music*.

'I also went on to work with Ronnie Barker a lot in *The Two Ronnies*, including in the film *The Picnic*, playing the maid who disappears inside a four-poster bed at the beginning of the picnic before coming out giggling. I also did all the girls' voices. I remember Ronnie joking to me one day. He claimed I was lucky my surname began with B because he often cast me after getting tired trawling through *Spotlight* [the actors' directory] – he'd return towards the front of the book and say: "She'll do."'

Nowadays Patricia appears mostly in dramas, such as *Holby City* and *Midsomer Murders*. Her appearances in the theatre are less frequent. 'I get tired of traipsing around the country, so rarely consider anything that takes me away from home for long periods.'

Isobel

Fletcher's wife, Isobel, to whom he was married for twenty-four years, was seen just once during *Porridge*. She appeared briefly in 'Men without Women', seemingly elated upon seeing her hubby return home on compassionate leave. We then discover they had cooked up a scheme between them to effect the leave: claiming their marriage was on the rocks, Fletch soft-soaped the prison's management into allowing him time to try and patch things up with his wife; what the Governor didn't realise was that he'd pulled a similar trick while serving time at Maidstone.

The irony of Fletch's scheming is that his life is soon tainted by marital problems. When he leaves prison, he discovers that Isobel (who was manager of a dry cleaner's)

has embarked on a new life of luxury in Chingford with the affluent Reg Jessop, owner of a cardboard-box factory off London's North Circular.

Fletch and Isobel were nineteen when they tied the knot, and – except in 1955, when he was King of the Teds and had a brief fling with Gloria, a machinist from a local clothing factory – he's been devoted to his Isobel.

Isobel was played by Jone Ellis, who has been seen in numerous other shows on television over the years. Her credits include *Out of the Unknown* and *The Prisoner* during the 1960s and *Faulty Towers* and *All Creatures Great and Small* in the seventies; *French and Saunders*, *Alas Smith and Jones*, *KYTV*, *An Affair in Mind* and *The Silver Chair* have followed since.

In films, she's played Brenda in 1960's *The Night of the Big Heat*, a blonde in 1967's *Quatermass and the Pit*, Bess in *Anne of the Thousand Days* and Mrs Wagstaffe in *Getting It Right*.

Marion

We never get to see Fletch's youngest daughter, Marion, but we hear plenty about her from Ingrid. She flits from job to job, beginning with one at Timothy White's, then selling shirts around the city's offices, before moving to Woolies. Fletch holds a low opinion of Marion, classing her as 'lazy'. He also dislikes her boyfriend, Ricky, whose wealth stems from running his own company, Sunset Tours, offering cheap charter flights.

By the time Fletcher returns home in *Going Straight*, Marion has been living away from home for two years, sharing a Maida Vale flat with some nurses.

Raymond

Fletcher's only son, Raymond, resides in a world of his own. When the series begins, he's just started grammar school, turning up for his first day in a uniform his father stole from a school-outfitters. But Fletch's absence during his son's form-ative years has had a detrimental effect: at fourteen,

Raymond smokes thirty cigarettes a day, although there's always the possibility his habit stems from the responsibility bestowed upon him in his role as stage manager of the school play.

He may be two years older and in his final term at school when we see him for the first time in *Going Straight*, but he remains as gormless as ever. Fletcher even remarks that he needs a new battery and must have been educated in lethargy.

Nicholas Lyndhurst was seventeen when he landed the role of Raymond. Born in Emsworth, West Sussex, he attended London's Corona Drama Academy from the age of ten. He stayed eight years, paying his fees from money earned making commercials. His first television work was for BBC Schools productions, and was followed by more expansive roles: in the period drama *Anne of Avonlea*, a leading role in the BBC's adaptation of *Heidi*, and, aged fourteen, the lead in *The Prince and the Pauper*.

But his big break came in the shape of Adam Parkinson in Carla Lane's highly rated sitcom *Butterflies* in 1978. Four series were made and by the time the closing episode was transmitted, five years later, Nicholas's was a familiar face to TV viewers across the nation.

Now, in his thirties, Nicholas's impressive list of credits also includes the role of Gary Sparrow in *Goodnight Sweetheart* and, in arguably his best performance to date, playing Rodney in *Only Fools and Horses*.

GOING STRAIGHT   GOING HOME

Original transcription: **Friday 24 February 1978**
BBC1, 8.30 p.m.

CAST

Norman Fletcher	**Ronnie Barker**
Mr Mackay	**Fulton Mackay**
McLaren	**Tony Osoba**
Mr Kirby	**Milton Johns**
Mr Collinson	**Paul McDowell**
Oaksie	**Timothy Bateson**
Tanner	**Norman Jones**
Scotcher	**Michael Turner**
Steward	**Bunny May**

Fletcher returns to the outside world and is determined to go straight. But just when he thinks he's free from the nightmare of Slade Prison, he bumps into Mr Mackay on the train south. They get chatting and it transpires that Mackay is travelling to the Smoke in search of a new job after twenty-five years with the prison service.

At Stafford, a couple of criminals jump on the train. They're on the run after robbing a jewellery shop and desperate to find an innocent bystander to relieve them of their loot until they're free from the pursuing police. Oaksie, one of the criminals, tells his boss to leave the bag with Fletch.

A case of mistaken identity finds Mackay lumbered with the bag of stolen property, much to Fletcher's amusement. Just when he's got the chance to land Mackay in trouble, Fletch remembers he's decided to turn over a new leaf and gets his ex-foe out of a tricky situation.

WHAT A SCENE!

Fletcher is preparing to leave prison, and chats with McLaren.

FLETCHER
D'you know, if there were two things I could take away from this prison as souvenirs, d'you know what they'd be?

MCLAREN
What?

FLETCHER
I'll give you a clue, they both belong to Mr Mackay.

GOING STRAIGHT — GOING TO BE ALRIGHT

Original transmission: **Friday 3 March 1978**
BBC1, 8.30 p.m.

CAST

Norman Fletcher	**Ronnie Barker**
Lennie Godber	**Richard Beckinsale**
Ingrid Fletcher	**Patricia Brake**
Shirley Chapman	**Rowena Cooper**
Raymond	**Nicholas Lyndhurst**
Householder	**Michael Stainton**
Builder	**Norman Hartley**

Fletcher is resolved to keep straight but he's finding it tough adjusting to life outside, especially as his wife, Isobel, has left him for a life of luxury with Reg Jessop, a cardboard-box manufacturer. Fletch has his first appointment with his probation officer, Shirley Chapman, who's disappointed to hear his refusal to accept Reg Jessop's job offer at his cardboard-box factory. She'll have to fix him up instead.

Short of cash, Fletch announces to his daughter Ingrid that a few years ago he buried thousands of pounds in a turnip field in Essex. But when she learns it is stolen money, she doesn't want anything to do with it. Fletcher, though, could do with an upturn in his luck and decides it's worth recovering; he sets out with his spade to unearth his fortune, only to find that new houses have been built on top of the site!

WHAT A SCENE!

Ingrid enquires as to what sort of day her dad has had.

INGRID

I said what sort of day have you had?

FLETCHER

Oh, not bad. I popped in to The White Hart for a swift half; then I had a pint and a pie in The Anchor, signed on, of course, at the labour and then I popped in The Magpie for a swift half, and then I went down to The Old Ship for a swift half en route to The Rainbow Club.

INGRID

Why did you go down The Rainbow?

FLETCHER

It's all that walking about, it made me thirsty.

Original transmission: 📺 **Friday 10 March 1978**
BBC1, 8.30 p.m.

CAST

Norman Fletcher	**Ronnie Barker**
Ingrid	**Patricia Brake**
Raymond	**Nicholas Lyndhurst**
Penny	**Roberta Tovey**
Dante	**Freddie Earlle**
Perce	**Ron Pember**
Arthur	**Dave Hill**

Fletcher's a forty-five-year-old ex-lag with no money, no job and no wife, and his situation is dragging him down. He feels his prospects are as exciting as 'a wet Sunday in Merthyr Tydfil', and to make matters worse he sees nothing but an untrustworthy, cynical world around him.

While Ingrid works as a manicurist, Fletch's daily routines involve doing the shopping and stopping for a quick cuppa at Dante's Café, where he becomes a crime-stopper. As Perce, the local milkman, counts his takings, a girl tries slipping her hand into his moneybag. But Fletcher spots the incident and steps in just in time to prevent her committing the dirty deed.

Feeling the loud-mouthed degenerate's need is greater than his, he plays the Good Samaritan by giving her his cuppa and a stick of Kit-Kat. Before long, Fletch's hospitality extends to inviting her home for a hot bath and a wholesome meal.

When he discovers she's run away from home, Fletcher's altruistic tendencies take over and he tries giving her some free advice; the last thing Fletch wants is to see a girl heading for a life like his, which has involved eleven years behind bars.

Sadly, his admirable intentions appear to backfire when Penny swipes Ingrid's purse from her handbag, but a final gesture from the girl helps restore Fletch's faith in human nature.

215

WHAT A SCENE!

Fletch is getting depressed about the cynical, untrusting world he's encountered since his release.

INGRID

Now you mustn't let things get on top of you – you never have.

FLETCHER

I know. I didn't think it was going to be as hard as this, that's all. I want to make myself useful, you know, I want to have a job, but with my record.

INGRID

Now that's not true. There's over a million unemployed in this country. There's boys what left Raymond's school two years ago who don't know nothing else but a dole queue.

FLETCHER

But it's this attitude of cynicism and mistrust I keep coming up against, which in turn makes me more cynical and that's something I've always resisted, you know that very well, don't ya? I mean I went into the Post Office the other day just to get a Postal Order for my pools; they've got a four-penny Biro chained to the wall. I mean, it still didn't write but it was chained to the wall.

INGRID

Well that's normal these days, Dad, it's the mood of the country.

GOING STRAIGHT — GOING TO WORK

Original transmission: **Friday 17 March 1978**
BBC1, 8.30 p.m.

CAST

Norman Fletcher . . . . **Ronnie Barker**
Lennie Godber . . . . **Richard Beckinsale**
Ingrid . . . . **Patricia Brake**
Mr McEwan . . . . **David Swift**
Shirley Chapman . . . . **Rowena Cooper**
Pamela . . . . **Elizabeth Cassidy**
Alfie . . . . **Eric Francis**
Vic . . . . **Stephen Tate**

Thanks to Mrs Chapman at the probation service, Fletch is fixed up with a job at the Dolphin Hotel, where the owner, Mr McEwan, helps ex-convicts get that all-important break upon release. For Fletch the idea of working takes some getting used to, partly because it's his first ever job – something Godber, who's dating Ingrid, finds highly amusing.

Fletch claims that he accepted the job to prove to the world – and to his family – that he could gain employment, but when he starts having second thoughts about turning up, Godber and Ingrid supply a helping hand.

WHAT A SCENE!

Godber discusses Fletch's new job.

GODBER

It must be your first legitimate job in . . . how long is it?

FLETCHER

Ever.

GODBER

(Laughs) What? Straight up, you've never had a job in your life?

FLETCHER

No, not unless you count the army.

INGRID

Which we don't because you were on the fiddle even then. D'you know, when I was a nipper all my party dresses were made out of parachute silk.

FLETCHER

You wouldn't have complained if you'd ever fallen out of a window, would you?

GOING STRAIGHT — GOING, GOING, GONE

Original transmission: 📺 **Friday 24 March 1978**
BBC1, 8.25 p.m.

CAST

Norman Fletcher	**Ronnie Barker**
Lennie Godber	**Richard Beckinsale**
Ingrid	**Patricia Brake**
Mr McEwan	**David Swift**
Giles	**Donald Morley**
Wellings	**Nigel Hawthorne**
Mrs Appleby	**Lally Bowers**
Raymond	**Nicholas Lyndhurst**
Crowther	**Peter Postlethwaite**
Nulty	**Martin Milman**

It's two months since Fletch's release and he's settled into his job as night porter at a local hotel. When a man arrives at the hotel, Fletch recognises the face but can't place his name. An old woman soon follows and deposits expensive jewellery in the safe, and Fletch's memory rushes back: the mystery man is Wellings, an ex-con with whom he served time. He's a con man who, along with an old woman, worked the south coast. While the old dear distracted the porter, Wellings would rob the safe, pretend the jewellery had been stolen and then claim off the insurance. Fletch takes matters into his own hands – but soon gets into difficulties.

WHAT A SCENE!

Ingrid contemplates marrying Godber.

GODBER

I've got a lot in common with your dad, haven't I?

INGRID

Unfortunately, yes. That's always going to embarrass me, that is. I mean, when we live somewhere nice people are going to ask me how I met my husband. And I'm going to have to say: 'He shared a cell with my dad.'

GOING OFF THE RAILS

GOING STRAIGHT

Original transmission: Friday 7 April 1978
BBC1, 8.30 p.m.

CAST

Norman Fletcher . . . . **Ronnie Barker**
Lennie Godber . . . . **Richard Beckinsale**
Ingrid . . . . **Patricia Brake**
Pybus . . . . **Alfred Lynch**
Police Sergeant . . . . **Royston Tickner**
Police Inspector . . . . **Robert Raglan**
Mrs Gilchrist . . . . **Gwyneth Owen**
Man . . . . **Norman Scace**
Shop Assistant . . . . **Val McCrimmon**
Registrar . . . . **Bill Horsley**
Raymond . . . . **Nicholas Lyndhurst**

After participating in an identity parade, Fletch meets an old acquaintance, Dave Pybus, a man with a camelhair coat, white tie and flashy motor. Dave offers to push some business Fletch's way, but he declines because he's going to go straight. In case Fletch changes his mind, Pybus leaves him his business card.

With Ingrid's wedding to Godber looming, Fletch wants to discuss arrangements – not that he's got much spare cash to help finance the event. It seems everything has been sorted, but upon discovering that his estranged wife's wealthy lover, Reg Jessop, is financing the reception at a plush establishment in Stanmore, Fletch takes umbrage.

Strapped for cash, Fletch has second thoughts about Dave Pybus' offer to earn a fast buck. Acting as lookout will bag him £500, and, although the work is on the morning of Ingrid's wedding, he'll be finished in time for the big occasion. It seems too good to refuse, but when Fletch enters a pet shop and recalls life behind bars, he pulls out of the job just in time for his daughter's nuptials.

WHAT A SCENE!

Fletch meets an old acquaintance, Dave Pybus, and over a drink they discuss their differing fortunes.

FLETCHER

To look at you, Dave, I wouldn't say you were exactly on your uppers. I mean that whistle, the car you drove us here in: automatic, two-tone, real leather upholstery, wing mirrors.

PYBUS

No, I'm thinking of changing it. Well it's coming up to 20,000. And my bloke, you know what puts the spanners to it, he says: 'Dave, best to do it now before something big goes like the gearbox.'

FLETCHER

Yes, I know what you mean, yes, I have the same problem with my bike. I've got to trade that in before the bell drops off.

PRODUCTION TEAM

ALL EPISODES WRITTEN BY
Dick Clement and Ian La Frenais

SIGNATURE TUNE WRITTEN BY
Tony Macauley and Dick Clement

FILM CAMERAMAN
Reg Pope
(all episodes except 'Going Sour')

FILM EDITOR
Bill Wright
(all episodes except 'Going Sour')

FILM SOUND
Ron Blight
(all episodes except 'Going Sour')

MAKE-UP
Christine Walmesley-Cotham

COSTUMES
Mary Husband

LIGHTING
John Dixon

SOUND
Richard Chamberlain

VIDEOTAPE EDITOR
John Turner (episodes 1–2 & 5);
Matt Boney (episode 3);
Roger Harvey (episodes 4 & 6)

PRODUCTION ASSISTANT
Mike Crisp

DESIGNER
Tim Gleeson

PRODUCER/DIRECTOR
Sydney Lotterby

222

A-Z OF PERIPHERAL CHARACTERS

APPEARING IN *PORRIDGE* AND *GOING STRAIGHT*

Only characters that have not been profiled in more depth
elsewhere in the book are listed in this chapter.

Pilot (Prisoner and Escort)

The Prison Warder (Hamish Roughead) works at Brixton Prison and hands Fletcher over to Mackay and Barrowclough when he's transferred to Slade Prison.

Porridge (Series One) – A Day Out

The Landlord (Ralph Watson) works at the pub frequented by Fltecher and Mackay.

The Nurse (Peggy Mason) is a district nurse who cycles past the prisoners while they're digging their ditches.

The VICAR (Robert Gillespie) is seen in the village pub when Mackay pops in for a drink.

The Verger (John Rutland) accompanies the Vicar to the local pub before heading back to the church once he hears prisoners are working on the moors.

Porridge (Series One) – Men without Women

Elaine (Rosalind Elliot) is Warren's beloved who is seen on visiting day.

Iris (Andonia Katsaros) is Heslop's wife, who arrives on visiting day.

Sergeant Norris (Royston Tickner) accompanies Fletcher to his home when he's granted forty-eight hours' compassionate leave after hearing his wife has, supposedly, found someone else.

Trevor (Donald Groves) is Lukewarm's partner who comes calling on visiting day. He's a watch repairer from Southport.

Norma (Susan Littler) is Tolly's wife who visits him in prison.

Porridge (Series Two) – No Peace for the Wicked

Prison Visitors (Ivor Roberts, Barbara New, Geoffrey Greenhill) are Home Office officials given a tour of the prison by Mackay.

Porridge (Series One) – No Way Out

The NURSE (Elisabeth Day) is employed at the hospital Fletch visits for a knee examination.

Sandra (Carol Hawkins) is a London girl who dresses up as a nurse in order to pass on a blank passport to Fletch while he attends hospital.

Going Straight – Going Home

Mr Kirby (Milton Johns) is the prison officer who returns Fletch's possessions upon his release. He's a miserable character: Fletcher remarks that he's never seen him smile.

Oaksie (Timothy Bateson) meets Fletcher on the train he catches upon his release. Cloth-capped Oaksie boards the train at Stafford.

Mr Scotcher (Michael Turner) is a policeman in the Flying Squad who once collared Fletcher. He boards Fletcher's train and is on the hunt for thieves who broke into a jeweller's. Believing the stolen goods are still on board, he questions Fletcher.

Steward (Bunny May) is the steward on the train Fletcher catches after being released from prison.

Mr Tanner (Norman Jones) joins the train with Oaksie at Stafford. Claims he was a major in the army – but, being as he's a criminal, it's uncertain. When he wants a bag delivered in London, because he's getting off at Watford, he confuses Mackay for Fletcher and persuades the prison officer to do the dirty deed.

Going Straight – Going to Be Alright

Householder (Michael Stainton) owns the house built on top of the money Fletcher buried a few years ago. He sees Fletch with his spade and ends up hiring him to dig a pond.

Shirley Chapman (Rowena Cooper) is Fletch's probation officer at the Muswell Hill office. They meet twice a week and she helps find him a job at the Dolphin Hotel. She's married with two kids, but her spouse, who's an aerospace engineer, is currently unemployed.

Man in Probation Office (Norman Hartley) is sitting waiting at the probation office when Fletcher arrives for his first meeting. It turns out he's a painter and decorator, there to provide a quote for giving the depressing office a fresh lick of paint.

Going Straight – Going Sour

Arthur Boyle (Dave Hill) arrives at the end of the episode to take Penny to Portsmouth and return the purse she'd pinched from Ingrid's handbag. Arthur is Penny's mother's partner.

Dante (Freddie Earlle) owns Dante's Café, where Fletch visits. States he comes from Sicily but Fletch knows better and reminds him his roots are in Stoke Newington.

Penny (Roberta Tovey) is spotted by Fletcher in the café trying to pinch money from the local milkman's moneybag. Fletch tries leading her back on to the straight and narrow with some fatherly advice. She used to live in Camberwell but when her mother moved to Portsmouth, together with her partner, Penny ran away from home. Her intention was to live with a friend, Pauline Soper, but her plans fell through. She eventually ends up moving to Pompey.

Perce (Ron Pember) is the local milkman who's counting his takings in the café when Fletcher arrives. Unknowingly, he's nearly a victim of crime when Penny tries grabbing his moneybag. Claims he's a happily married man when Fletch enquires about his rendezvous with a lady nearby.

The Policeman (not credited) pops into Dante's Café while Fletcher is there with Penny. From the girl's reaction, Fletch realises she's on the run from the police and befriends her.

Going Straight – Going to Work

Alfie (Eric Francis) is the barman at The Black Lion, Fletch's local.

Mr McEwan (David Swift) owns the Dolphin Hotel where Fletch works as a night porter. A bearded man who spent many years in Malawi, McEwan likes helping the local probation service by offering employment to convicts upon release.

Pamela (Elizabeth Cassidy) is the secretary-cum-receptionist at the Dolphin Hotel who's a little sceptical about Mr McEwan's policy of employing ex-cons.

Vic (Stephen Tate) leaves the pub just as Fletch enters.

Going Straight – Going, Going, Gone

Mrs Appleby (Lally Bowers) is staying in room 2 at the Dolphin Hotel. When she asks Fletcher to put her necklace in the safe, he thinks she's in partnership with Mr Wellings and is planning to defraud the insurance company. But he's wrong: the wealthy grey-haired old lady is genuine and has visited the hotel for years. Her son works in the theatre while her late hubby used to own a toffee company.

Cheryl (Rikki Howard) is the blonde who accompanies Giles, who mistakenly calls her Beryl, into the Dolphin Hotel.

Thomas Clifford Crowther (Peter Postlethwaite),

formerly serving with the West End Central police force, is now working with the Flying Squad. He stops to chat with Fletch just round the corner from the Dolphin Hotel.

Giles (Donald Morley) arrives at the Dolphin Hotel late one night with a young blonde called Cheryl. Smiling like a Cheshire cat, he asks for a room, claiming his car has broken down, the blonde is his wife and he's decided to stay the night, although it's clear he wants the room for a little hanky-panky.

Nulty (Martin Milman) works for Crowther in the Flying Squad. Upon spotting Fletcher, they get out of their Ford Granada to find out what he's up to. Whilst doing so their car is pinched.

Mr Wellings (Nigel Hawthorne) has room 26 at the Dolphin Hotel. He's a former conman who served time with Fletcher at Maidstone. Used to work with an old woman along the south coast in places like Bournemouth and Torquay, submitting false insurance claims. But Wellings has been straight for six years and works as a bathroom-tile salesman.

Going Straight – Going Off the Rails

Mrs Gilchrist (Gwyneth Owen) is the woman who's asked to try and identify a suspect at the identity parade, but fails to pick anyone because the person she's looking for is ginger-haired.

The Man (Norman Scace) is a bespectacled man, standing in the identity parade, who Fletcher annoys.

The Police Inspector (Robert Raglan) ushers Mrs Gilchrist to the identity parade.

The Police Sergeant (Royston Tickner) helps co-ordinate the identity parade at the police station. He knows Fletch.

Dave Pybus (Alfred Lynch) knows Fletch from years gone by and offers him the chance to earn £500 as a lookout during a forth-coming job he's arranging.

Rather ostentatious, Pybus used to frequent Fletch's old local, The Hand and Flower, and now runs a business manufacturing party novelties, while his other work is rather less legal.

The Registrar (Bill Horsley) marries Ingrid and Godber.

The Shop Assistant (Val McCrimmon) works in a pet shop that Fletch enters pretending he's buying a dog for Ingrid's wedding present. But when all the cages start reminding him of prison, he leaves.